HOMELESS
BUT LIFE IN
A SHELTER
HUMAN

First Edition, October 2018
Blue Byron Books
Chicago, Illinois

Editing: Shayla Raquel, ShaylaRaquel.com
Publishing and Design Services: Melinda Martin, MelindaMartin.me
Book Cover: Mariana Krasteva
Author Photo: Alexis Pedroza

ISBN 978-1-7326882-0-9 (pbck), 978-1-7326882-1-6 (epub)

HOMELESS

BUT LIFE IN A SHELTER

HUMAN

RICH HEBRON

*To those willing to follow their curiosity
and challenge their perspective.*

CONTENTS

PREFACE

Every night at the homeless shelter, I scribbled words and quotes into a small memo pad. Though barely legible and written in the dark, they were enough to trigger my memory of events and conversations when I typed them in a Google doc the next day or two later at the library.

When I returned from living homeless, nine months passed before I read my journal. I was afraid to read it. *What if my experience wasn't what I thought?* I couldn't handle that. But I needed to find out. I read it, smiling and shedding tears the entire time. I wanted to share it with others, but it needed work. This book is a product of reflection and revision over six years.

I hope my experience can provide another perspective on homelessness—one different than you're used to. To solve the biggest problems of our time, we need to listen and learn from others' lives, experiences, and perspectives. Sometimes it helps to take an unconventional approach.

CHAPTER ONE

YOU'RE GOING TO DO WHAT?

Pop! Reid pulled the cork from the bottle of red wine. He poured two glasses half full and raised one to his nose, closed his eyes, and sniffed.

"Mhm. Mhm. Mhm." He bobbed his head, letting the experience of the wine marinate.

His studio apartment was small. I sat on the pullout sofa, and he sat on a wicker chair. He owned few things but placed them meticulously. A dark-brown shelf held ten books or so—books I could barely wrap my head around, written by philosophers and economists. He remarked that he had started collecting antique Bibles and pointed to three tattered leather books. Reid dabbled in photography—well, enough to display two photos and convince guests he dabbled in photography. One photo was a bottle of Cristal, which he and five other friends shared the previous New Year's. The other was the sunset behind the Milwaukee skyline, the city where he spent four years going to school.

Reid was the smartest person I knew, even though he was only two years older than me. We became friends in high school and competed on the forensics team, winning trophies and medals against other teenage public speakers in Wisconsin. Our conversations quickly veered into philosophical and "changing the world" directions. They evoked a curiosity inside me.

That night, he dove into the topic of quantum mechanics.

"I'm telling you, we're going to be able to teleport!" He threw one hand in the air and balanced his glass of wine in the other. "But it won't happen in our lifetimes, probably like two hundred fifty years or so." I smirked. He held up a thick book. "It's in this book right here. You see, the universe . . ."

I zoned out quickly, but I did my best to nod along, pretending to be engaged and captivated. Honestly, science didn't interest me much, but I appreciated its importance.

Deeper into our bottle of wine, an hour later, we ordered pizza. We devoured two-thirds of it but hit a wall.

"What should we do with the rest of it? I'd hate to throw it out," I said, rubbing my too-full belly.

He shrugged. "I don't know. Give it to one of the homeless guys that hangs out a few blocks away."

I furrowed my brow. "Would they even want someone's scraps? Isn't that kind of shitty of us to just assume?" Our conversation steered into the issue of homelessness.

The truth was, we didn't know much about it. We both lived in large cities since high school. Seeing homeless people in Chicago was unavoidable—begging for change at intersections, guiding carts through alleyways, or standing in lines outside soup kitchens. It was always there, around us, yet vague.

"Hmm." He scratched his head, peering to the ceiling for answers. "What if someone were to voluntarily live homeless?"

"Like on the streets?" I leaned forward and pushed up my glasses. "Yeah."

"Can you do that? Is that allowed?" I asked.

"I don't know. I've never really heard about anyone doing it. But I'm not talking about like a night or even a week—*longer*." I leaned back again, crossed my arms, and listened to Reid. "I've seen a pastor or two do it for a night or two, then come out 'transformed.' Some churches do like a 'night on the streets' where they camp out to build solidarity for the homeless and try to empathize. Don't get me wrong—that's a good thing. But it's bullshit." He tapped his fingers on the coffee table. "What I'm talking about is getting dirty, immersing oneself in the community—having a routine and taking on emotions like others."

"How long do you think that'd take?" I asked, genuinely intrigued by the thought.

"I don't know. A month? Maybe a few months? I really have no idea. But imagine if someone did something like that. It'd provide a unique perspective to consider." He leaned to the other side of his chair, getting more comfortable. "I mean, think how our perspective on the homeless usually develops: we awkwardly interact on the sidewalk, governments tell us numbers and statistics—policies and initiatives, they say, have helped communities—and nonprofits tell us how hopeless people are. It'd be interesting to hear a different perspective—one that doesn't view them with pity or as numbers.

For as much as large-scale, financially bolstered campaigns and programs create change, so do ideas."

My curiosity took notice. I began envisioning what living homeless would be like. Nervous butterflies fluttered inside me. *Could I pull off an unthinkable quest like that?* Learning how it felt to live homeless appealed to me most, especially as someone studying communication and psychology. *What goes through a person's mind when sleeping in a park or shelter? What about when they beg for money on the streets? But what about the risks?*

"So what potential dangers do you think could come up?" I asked Reid.

"Well, you could get stabbed or shot! Not to mention illnesses." My stomach dropped. "You could come out pretty fucked up psychologically," he added. "Who knows . . . some guys might like it and want to stay."

I lowered my eyebrows with a disbelieving smile. "You think that could happen if someone lived *voluntarily* homeless?"

"Sure. Why not? It's a possibility." Reid was always levelheaded, so I should've expected that answer. "There's also the other questions."

"What do you mean?"

"Ethically." He scratched his chin, enjoying this deep conversation more than ever. It dove into philosophy. It wasn't black and white any longer. "Voluntarily living homeless would be controversial. Would someone be taking away resources from others?" he posed rhetorically to me. "People would wonder about the genuineness. If you could *theoretically* leave your homeless situation when you felt like it, would the experience be authentic? Issues of privilege arise."

I broke my stare and looked at the ceiling. "Hmm." That was an unintended consequence I hadn't thought of. My mind worked harder to grasp the question. I looked around the apartment. Two empty wine bottles sat on the coffee table. His clock read 10:45. Time had escaped us.

Reid continued, "The background of someone voluntarily living homeless might be different than someone who became homeless because, say, the loss of a job," he said.

"Yeah, I can understand that." I paused. "But how do we know the answers to these questions and ideas if we don't try?"

"Aha!" Reid gestured with his index finger. "That's the more appropriate question to ask." He was fully engaged now. "The truth is, humans want what's easy. They don't want to dig deeper if they don't have to, because it's uncomfortable and takes effort. Society moves slowly, protecting itself by dismissing those who dare to think outside of it. If someone lived voluntarily homeless, the knee-jerk reaction would be to reject it, under the guise that someone from a more privileged background couldn't possibly understand someone without."

"Well, how do you progress without getting uncomfortable?"

"You don't," he said.

Our conversation paused. I focused on his eyes. "I'm gonna do it."

His body straightened. "Mhm. Mhm. Mhm." He bobbed his head but didn't say anything. He read so many books that theorizing became second nature to him. Taking action on the idea was something different to him, though. He stared blankly, as if his mind began envisioning the application. I didn't think he believed me—I didn't blame him. But more importantly, he didn't dismiss me.

———

So why *wouldn't* I voluntarily live homeless? Because it'd be too tough? Anything worthwhile was tough. Because it'd be potentially dangerous? I was twenty-one years old. Danger was an abstract idea I hardly knew. Because I'd have to get dirty? I grew up on a farm. Dirt was nothing. Because of my student loans? Uncle Sam waited six months after graduation before knocking on my door for his money. If still homeless, preparing a couple payments could be done. Because it could mess me up psychologically? Yeah, right.

Gaining an enlightened perspective on a marginalized community, seemingly so misunderstood by society, energized me. The redundant images and stereotypes of homelessness bored me. There had to be more there, and I wanted to discover it. Maybe after, I could help others better understand it too.

Conformity never satisfied my curiosity. The American Dream was pounded into my head growing up by my parents and teachers. The idea intoxicated me. No matter where you started, you could achieve your dream with good ideas and hard work. In eighth grade, during Teacher Appreciation Week, quotes were taped to each student's locker. Mine read, "No one is a failure in the world who lightens the burden for another." I later looked it up and learned it was a variation of a Charles Dickens quote. But it's something I always remembered and wanted to live up to. I knew conforming wasn't the path to achieve it. I challenged my comfort zone, like risking social isolation by wearing my dad's suits and trading my backpack for a briefcase at my rural high school. Later, I left the farm for college in Chicago.

The nauseating term, *real world*, rammed itself into so many conversations my senior year of college. I didn't want to start climbing the rungs of society's ladder like my peers. I knew living homeless, to better understand how it felt, would enrich my perspective more than any entry-level job.

———

My family held a graduation party for me in late June and after my relatives and friends left, I pulled aside my parents.

"I know I haven't told you my plans. I wanna go over them with you," I said.

"Of course!" They responded with a cheery eagerness. Smiles lit up their faces. As the sun set in our backyard, we walked inside the house to our kitchen table.

I was a first-generation college graduate. It was a huge deal to my parents. My mom stayed at home to raise my three siblings and me. My dad worked for the county highway department and the family farm his whole life. My dad, especially, encouraged me to earn good grades and be involved with extracurricular school activities because he never had a chance to. When I was younger, I rode in the tractor cab with him, and we had conversations about my future. He pushed me to keep working hard so I wouldn't have to live paycheck to paycheck. He believed a college degree was a ticket to a more financially secure life. I took that to heart and wanted to make him proud.

We all sat down at the table. I pulled a piece of paper from my pocket. I had a speech. I thought delivering an organized monologue would be the easiest way to disseminate the news that I'd be living homeless.

But suddenly, my hands shook violently. The piece of paper moved around like it was caught in storm winds. Tears rushed down my face. Shock paralyzed my body. I couldn't speak. I didn't know what was happening to me. I had never experienced a loss of control of my body like this. Words fumbled out of my mouth.

"Ca-can we d-do th-this t-tomorrow?" I gulped, trying to swallow my emotions.

"Are you all right?" my mom asked.

"Y-yeah," I said. I often had trouble communicating my feelings to my parents. I didn't want to look weak. I didn't want to show vulnerability to my parents. I thought it would make them question themselves as parents, which I didn't want them to do because I loved them.

They didn't push me further. They smiled and nodded.

The following night, composed and determined, I delivered my speech. I expressed why I chose to do it. I wanted to learn more about the homeless community, who it affected, and how it felt.

I was curious. It ended something like, "I believe that sharing my perspective might help others better understand the issue."

Now *my* parents' bodies sat paralyzed instead of mine. My mother's mouth fell open, gasping for air. Tears gushed from her eyes, streaming down her pale face. She dipped her chin and covered her eyes with her hand and shook her head in resentment. After all, they had made sacrifices for me, and this was how I treated them?

My dad, equally surprised, responded differently. A dazed stare stretched across his face. He didn't say anything. He concentrated on the news and tried processing the appropriate response. He eventually copied my mother's weeping.

I wasn't doing what I was supposed to. People didn't attain a college degree to do something like I was planning. For most of my life, I believed the purpose of a college degree was to land a good job to enjoy a higher standard of living. It was a piece of paper that granted access to a higher class of American society. By the time I graduated, I thought differently. To me, attaining a college degree meant viewing the world more holistically, which allowed an individual the increased ability to create change in that same world. But society didn't share my point of view.

I remained seated, overwhelmed by guilt and sweating through my clothes as I watched my parents wrestle with intense emotional pain—all of which I alone created. I joined them in crying.

So, what would we do? Would I back out because it'd stress out my parents? That wasn't the solution. I made the decision a year before, and I believed the right thing to do was to include my parents. They deserved to know, as difficult as it was.

Most parents would've become furious. They would've tried to stop their child from living voluntarily homeless. My parents were different. They didn't like my decision—and I didn't even think they completely understood why I'd do it—but they supported me. It was my life, and it was my decision. My mother hugged me, and her tears soaked my clothes. My strong father cried in my arms, revealing a vulnerability I had never witnessed before. My head ached from the surreal situation. I never felt pain like that.

———

In the days and weeks ahead, I moved back to Wisconsin to spend time with my family. My parents grappled with the reality that their son would be living in the streets of Chicago. One evening, I sat at the family computer and my mom approached me. She asked me about the logistics of my living homeless. She tried to look courageous, but her closed lips and watering eyes deceived her. She acknowledged that my endeavor would soon be a reality. It was going to happen.

"Well, I'm just going to drop off the grid. I'm not bringing a phone with me," I asserted.

My mom shook her head. "Well, we need to be in contact with you somehow to know you're all right." I understood her practicality and desire to know I was safe.

"I'll have email access still, so I can keep you updated through that. But I'm only going to be in contact with you two—no one else." I didn't want anyone else to know where I was or what I'd be doing. Complications were more likely to occur with more people knowing; plus, rumors spread and original thoughts get lost. It wasn't a risk I wanted to take.

"What about your brother and sisters? Grandma and Grandpa? Everyone?" my mom inquired. "What will we tell them?"

"I told my friends in Chicago I'm backpacking through Europe and that I'm deactivating my Facebook because I'm going to write a book about our generation's addiction with digital technology."

"We can't tell our family that!" my mother retorted. "They won't believe it."

My face burned red and my cheeks ballooned. After a year of planning, it was the stupid logistics tripping me up.

"Why not? People do that!" I contested.

"Rich, you know that won't work." She raised her eyebrows in a lecturing, motherly way. What bothered me was that I knew she was right. I argued with her for the sake of arguing.

Cultural and class differences existed between people in rural Wisconsin and Chicago. Most of my Chicago friends came from middle-class backgrounds, from the suburbs and around the country, where graduating college was expected of them; whereas, in my community, a college degree was an option but certainly not mandated. It was blue-collar. To friends in college, exploring Europe was unconventional but somewhat understandable. My mom felt the explanation wouldn't work with friends and relatives.

"It has to be somewhere in the US," my mom said.

"Hawaii."

She rolled her eyes. "No."

"Well, it has to be far enough away where no one will think to visit me," I snapped back. "What about San Diego?"

She paused and rubbed her chin. "Yeah, I think that can work." We were finally on the same page. I exhaled in relief that it hadn't grown more complicated.

On August sixth, my parents drove me to the Metra train station in Waukegan, Illinois. My backpack rested on the seat next to me, overfilled with clothes, toiletries, a notebook, and other accessories.

My parents expressed their concerns as we neared the station.

"What will you do if something happens to a family member?" my mother asked me.

"Then I'll just deal with it when the time comes," I said as my father parked the car. I put my backpack on as we headed to the train, checking one last time that I had everything I'd need.

Hugs immediately ensued, and I heard the final call to board. Tears stained my T-shirt as my parents said their goodbyes. I climbed aboard the train and sat on the upper deck near a window. Mom and Dad waved, and I gave them a thumbs-up.

My stomach dropped as the train began its departure.

CHAPTER TWO

INSPIRED HORIZONS

I knocked on the red door. I stayed at the shelter two nights before. Strangely, no one was in sight. It was 4:45, the time a volunteer instructed me to return. I knocked once again and discovered the door was unlocked. I opened it a sliver. The door creaked.

"Hello?" I called.

Nothing.

"Hello?" I tried again. Footsteps rustled in the distance. I stepped back and waited.

A man wearing a hairnet greeted me with a southern twang. "Hey, what can I do for ya? I'm the cook here," he said.

"Well, I stayed here two nights ago," I explained. "On my way out in the morning, I asked someone what to do, and they told me to be back at this time."

The man hung his head and bit his lip. "I'm really sorry about that. It's not here that you're supposed to be at four forty-five—it's Inspired Horizons. That's where the program is. You sign in there.

Guys only come here at night."

I dimpled to one side. "Inspired Horizons?" I repeated.

"Yeah, it's about a mile south of here. Actually, if you hurry, you should be able to catch Lenny. When you get to this corner here"—he pointed out the door—"take a right until you get to Sheridan."

I nodded. "Uh huh."

"And then take a right again and just walk until you hit Wilson. Horizons is on Clifton, just west of the red line stop."

"Thanks!" I raced to Inspired Horizons.

———

Along the way, I reflected on living homeless for one month already. I used the first month to transition into the experience, like getting my feet wet or building a foundation.

It was pretty boring—well, at least during the day. Most of my time was spent *killing* time. The nights, though, were tough. If the weather forecast didn't have rain, I'd sleep (or try to) in parks. I never slept fully exposed, though, like on a park bench or building steps. My favorite spot was a small patch of woodchip bedding with surrounding trees along the fence line of the Lincoln Park Zoo. I rested the best there—although, there was that one time it downpoured unexpectedly. I sat on the ground curled up in a ball, holding my umbrella above my head for twenty minutes. It was only good until the middle of the night, when I routinely woke up shivering from the temperature drop. I then walked to a nearby building and army-crawled through its bushes for shelter. Of course, I learned to only do it after 3:30 a.m., the time when the sprinklers turned on. But other than that, I found that particular spot to be a more productive outdoor sleeping spot than others. The trees shielded me from people and harsh winds, and no urine stains suffocated my breathing.

When it did rain, however, finding shelter proved problematic. Roofed structures were available but not incredibly easy to find. Temperature drops still affected me, but this time, the rain kept me from walking to another spot to increase my blood flow. Indoor sleeping spots were better, but sneaking into churches and schools required swift decisions and then a high degree of patience—well, technically, I never sneaked into buildings; I just happened to be inside them when the last person locked the doors and left. Fortunately, I was only caught twice. The first time, I pretended to leave but hid somewhere else in the building. The second time was more interesting. When the custodian discovered me, he empathized with me and let me stay. He even gave me a box of Popeye's chicken tenders, fries, and a biscuit. I met a saint that night.

Originally, I brought an arbitrary amount of $146 with me. The first night, I bought a thirty-day CTA pass for eighty-five dollars. I figured once I burned through the rest, I'd eat in soup kitchens and beg on the streets. I ate at two soup kitchens. One was in Rogers Park, the northernmost neighborhood in the city, and the other in Uptown, a neighborhood on the north side. I didn't, however, beg for money. I already did so many uncomfortable things that I decided to postpone it, thinking it'd be a humiliating and awful experience. Instead, I memorized my checking account number and withdrew about twenty-five dollars each week. It was a conservative amount, so I never felt like I veered from my original intent. I planned to revisit the idea of begging once I joined a shelter program.

After one month, fatigue overwhelmed me. My hygiene dipped. I walked everywhere, developing blisters on my feet. And they never got air because I slept with my socks and shoes on. I bathed on Thursdays and Sundays, either by swimming in the lake with a bar of soap or showering in the park locker rooms. All other days, I smelled repulsive. Sometimes people jumped up when I sat next to them on the bus or at the library, which both embarrassed and humored me.

My fatigue was more mental than physical, though. I had never spent so much energy on the logistics of each day. Living homeless required conscious thinking and planning of mundane daily aspects. *Where do I wash my face in the morning? Where do I go to the bathroom? Where do I go to escape the rain? Where do I hang out without drawing much attention to myself? When do particular public and private spaces open and close? Where do I brush my teeth? Where do I sleep?* All that—and then never sleeping well. Each day dragged me along, not caring how exhausted I felt. The stress and mental drain carried over from the previous day, piling up inside.

My favorite part, if I had one, was the sunrise. Every morning, it provided hope. I struggled each night, but the sun didn't care. The sun provided positivity, tough love, a new day. It said, "You made it."

My loneliness surprised me the most. The same thoughts repeated over and over in my head. I entertained myself by carrying my own conversations and jokes aloud. I cherished interactions with others: a librarian answering a question of mine, a bus driver making a quip about a pedestrian in the street, a cute girl who flashed me a smile as she walked her dog—it didn't matter. Any interaction was thirst-quenching. I longed for companionship. Joining an overnight shelter was the next step toward reaching my goal, but at the same time, I hoped it'd curb my loneliness.

———

I reached Wilson Avenue and walked west, passing the deteriorating red line stop, its faded paint and rotted wood communicating what most of the city already knew: it was one of the worst red line stops. In the coming years, Chicago dedicated funds to rebuild the stop to make the area more attractive, though gentrification in Uptown was already progressing. A newly built Target was a block away, yet Harold's Chicken and storefronts of generic businesses like Communications and Taxes lined the littered streets. People stood on the streets, many asking for change as pedestrians walked by.

My eyes almost missed Clifton Avenue. It wasn't a typical-looking street—it was an alleyway. The parked cars, most of which looked two decades old, had orange tickets on their windshields, courtesy of the City of Chicago Department of Finance. Bikes missing their wheels were chained to street sign poles. Corroded fire escapes hung on the sides of the worn, brown-brick exteriors of industrial buildings—its heyday was long behind it.

A man with braids, aviator sunglasses, and a bright-yellow vest leaned against the wall under a brown awning with the words INSPIRED HORIZONS on it. He chewed on a toothpick and held his head toward the sky with an arrogance only someone on a power trip would have.

"What're you doing?" he yelled at me.

I stepped back and answered, "I'm looking for Lenny."

"Oh." His body loosened. He stuck his head inside the door and called for Lenny. He looked back at me and continued chewing on his toothpick. After about thirty seconds, which seemed longer to me, he lost his patience and walked inside the door and shouted, "Lenny! Someone's at the door!"

Moments later, a chubby black man wearing a green baseball cap walked toward us. "What can I do for you?" he asked me.

"I was just over at this shelter where I stayed two nights ago"—I pointed north—"and was told to show up again at four forty-five. When I got there, the cook told me to come here."

"Yes, this is Inspired Horizons. This is where the program is," he said. "We have two shelters for men. Unfortunately, there's no more room at the Gym tonight—the place you stayed—but you can go to Rawls, which is the sister shelter to Horizons, on the west side." My heart sank. I knew nothing other than that it was in an area I was unfamiliar with, and that more violence occurred on the west side than the north side.

Though hesitant, I decided to go with the flow. "Yeah, I'll go there."

"All right. You can hang out in the dayroom until the van comes. Follow me."

We walked together through a dimly lit hallway. "What's your name?" he asked.

"Rick," I replied. For the last month, I went by Rick instead of Rich, worried that an authority would Google my name and look into my background.

"Rick, I'm Lenny. I'm the case manager here. If you need something, let me know." He pointed to a faded door. "That's the bathroom right there." We continued walking. "That's the computer room if you need to look for resources." A piece of paper hung on the window of the door that read:

No Facebook or YouTube! If you are caught using these sites, you will be banned one week from the internet.

We arrived at a room filled with people. The table in front of us, and an area around it, was for staff.

"See that yellow line?" He pointed to a faded stripe on the concrete ground.

"Yeah?"

"That's where you stand for roll call. Every day at four forty-five, we read off names and then you can go across to the cafeteria. We lock the doors during dinner and open them again at five thirty," he informed me. "In the morning, come here and sign in before breakfast, which is at seven. The sign-in reserves your spot at the Gym. There're sixty beds and as long as you don't miss a day, you'll get the same bed, sheet, blanket, and pillow. Otherwise, you go on the overflow list. If someone doesn't show up for roll call, a guy on the overflow list can replace him. Understood?"

"Yeah." I nodded.

"All right then. The van for Rawls usually shows up at six. If you have an extra bag or want to keep something here, you can put it on there so you don't have to carry it around with you." He pointed to a large rack filled with beat-up suitcases, wrinkled plastic bags, and dirty duffle bags.

"Thanks," I replied. Lenny sat down at the staff table, and I explored the rest of the space known as the dayroom.

It was a small area with worn-down tables and chairs. The low ceiling made it feel more claustrophobic than it was. The wall opposite the rack had a colorful mural of the Chicago skyline, which contrasted the muted yellow, red, and brown colors found everywhere else. The Jumpman logo in the top right corner reminded me of the bat signal—Michael Jordan was Chicago's superhero.

A monstrous TV that looked like it required four grown men to move it sat on top of a table in the front of the room. Next to it on the wall, a yellow sign read U-Turns Allowed. A bookshelf of tattered books, including the 1995 Encyclopedia series, stood in the corner.

The pool table near the staff area used books stacked underneath its legs to keep its surface level. Below one corner pocket, a cardboard box caught balls. A sign, taped to a pole, read:

The pool table closes at 4:00 p.m. Keep this space clear for roll call.

I sat on an open chair near the rack and looked around. Loneliness reared itself again. The dayroom was crowded. Guys near the TV and at tables had conversations with the guys next to them, laughing and showing a companionship I wish I had. Their friendships intimidated me. Would I ever get to that level with anybody?

I hoped so, but it seemed daunting. I never thought about friendships in that way like I did in that moment. It wasn't that I lacked confidence in my ability to make friends; it was the vulnerability of starting at zero.

"Rawls! Rawls!" a staff member relayed.

"Gotta have balls to go to Rawls!" someone shouted. Others laughed.

"Yeah, you gotta have balls to go to Rawls!" another reinforced, shaking his head.

A few stared at me with worried looks as if they wondered if I'd survive the night.

What did they mean? Why would they say that? What were the people like at Rawls? Were they different than the guys who went to the Gym? I figured it would be in an even worse neighborhood than Inspired Horizons, but by how much? *What was the process like and how many guys stayed there? Could it really be so bad that it inspired its own catchy phrase?*

A couple guys stood up and made their way to a door. I followed them through an industrial garage, where smoking was allowed, thinking they'd lead me to the van Lenny told me about. The fewer number of guys made the air taste fresher, even with the haze of smoke. Guys sat around rickety metal tables in mismatched chairs: dining room chairs, fold-up chairs, broken lawn chairs, and even upside-down buckets.

"Gotta have balls to go to Rawls!" a guy said, leaning back in a lawn chair. He smiled and puffed out a cloud of smoke. I couldn't escape the phrase. I grew more curious about Rawls and what I'd encounter.

CHAPTER THREE

YOU GOTTA HAVE BALLS TO GO TO RAWLS

A crowd of guys gathered outside of a long, white van parked a hundred feet away in the alley. I meandered over with my hands in my pockets. A tall, spirited man with gold teeth, a thick beard, and a round belly started calling our names from the overflow list. A do-rag covered his wave hairstyle. One after the other, each man jumped aboard.

"You Rick?" he asked. I nodded. "Good. I'm Phil. I'll be takin' you on our journey today." He shoved a bottle of hand sanitizer into my hand. "Here! When you jack off, it'll make your shit smooth." My cheeks flushed and I murmured a thank-you as I took my seat on the van, bunched with the others.

We turned onto Ashland, heading south. Phil blasted old school R&B tracks through the speakers. The tall man sitting next to me knew every song. His name was Reggie; he was in his forties, had big ears, and wore a white T-shirt and a brown winter hat. On his right cheek, he had a gash-like scar. He sang along word for word and sometimes performed commentary.

"Yeah, there you go, Teena Marie! You sing it, girl! White girl can sing!"

"Rest in peace, Teena!" Phil added.

Phil and Reggie discussed her death. Phil constantly looked in the rearview mirror and turned his body back toward Reggie and me. He turned the volume down when he spoke and then turned it up when Reggie talked.

"That picture frame fucked her up! She was at that hotel, and it fell on her while she was sleepin'. Ain't that somethin'? I'll be damned if that's the way I go," Phil said. "Shoot! With my luck, though, I finna be walkin' down the street and trip over a crack in the sidewalk. They'll say, 'Here lies that fool who couldn't even walk down a street without killin' himself.'"

"I'mma die in bed with two women," Reggie declared. "They'll say, 'Here lies the man whose heart stopped workin' 'cause he gave out too much lovin'.'" The rest of the guys in the van laughed.

Phil tried topping Reggie. "We'll, I'll finna say, 'Come here, ladies. Console yourselves about that poor man's death.'"

"Oh, no you ain't! I'm gonna haunt you," Reggie assured Phil.

"Phil, look to your right." Reggie pointed to a group of girls at an intersection. We passed another woman, and Reggie's head turned and he stared until she disappeared in the distance. "Some girls in Chicago are so pretty that I'm too afraid to talk to them." He quivered and popped his chest back out. "But shoot! Back when I had more money, I'd go to the strip clubs. There's Chandelier's downtown—lots of white hoes there. I'd grab like four hundred dollars and throw down two hundreds." Using his whole body, he spoke so animatedly that he almost pushed me off the bench. "I'd get some head and bust a nut; then, I'd go home and get head from my girl and bust a nut. I would sleep like a little baby." He laid his head on his folded hands. "But you can only go so long before the light shines on you, though."

The rest of the guys grunted in agreement.

Reggie's extraversion helped cure his need for attention. He liked the spotlight. Everyone seemed to find him wildly entertaining, including myself. His personality and humor relaxed me. I didn't feel so nervous about going to Rawls now that Reggie was here.

"What's your name?" he asked me.

"Rick," I replied.

"Where you from?"

"Wisconsin."

"Oh, you a country boy, hey?"

I rubbed the back of my neck, the heat rising from my embarrassment. "Yeah, that's right."

"Well, we gonna teach you a few things about the city."

Phil parked the van in front of a small church. The men outside halted their conversations and stared at us, giving me an uneasy feeling. Phil jumped from the driver's seat and met us as we hopped, one by one, out of the vehicle.

"Here you go!" Phil said charismatically, handing every person a CTA card to return to Inspired Horizons the next morning.

Since I bought a thirty-day CTA each month, I put it in my

backpack and figured I'd save it.

The building was a faded tan color with brownish-red accents. Its triangular façade struck me as overly symmetrical, like someone learned about the concept and went overboard applying it. Two large, identical, wooden doors were on each side. The one on the left was for the church, and the one on the right was for the shelter, which opened at 7:00 p.m.

Guys began entering the shelter, so I joined them.

"Whoa, whoa, whoa, cowboy!" Reggie grabbed my shoulder. I rotated my head, confused by what he meant. "Wait a bit," he said. "Let a crowd go in front of you. The order you sign in is the order of the beds—and beds one through twenty have bed bugs. Ain't no way you wanna end up like those guys. Red marks and shit from bites."

My mouth fell open. "You serious?"

"Yeah. See, those beds are against the wall. And that wall has wood at the bottom. You feel me?"

"What about the other beds?" I asked, suddenly scratching my arms for no reason.

"You shouldn't have to worry," Reggie said, trying to calm me. "And there'll always be guys with no problem going first. It's an ego thing for a lot of 'em."

We entered and waited on a staircase. At the bottom, a volunteer and parole officer sat behind a small fold-up table. The sheet of paper had seventy-five slots. I signed my name next to thirty-four. Volunteers, I learned, were also homeless but by helping out with tasks throughout the night, they got small perks like skipping the dinner line or choosing which bed they wanted to sleep on.

"Grab your number there. That's your shower ticket," the volunteer with a blond ponytail instructed me. "Showers are mandatory. You wait in line and give that to Keon over there." He pointed toward the other end of the room.

Small, quarter-sized pieces of cardboard with numbers lay scattered on the table. Searching for number thirty-four was like trying to find a particular piece for a jigsaw puzzle. Finally, with guys piling up behind me in line, I found my ticket.

"If you have any cigarettes, lighters, or a love towel, hand it over for the night," another volunteer with a bulldog-looking underbite announced as he patted me down.

"What's that?" I asked. *Did he say what I thought he said? A love towel?*

The volunteer laughed, patting me on the shoulder. "Yeah, if you gotta rub one out, don't do it here. Do it somewhere else." I grimaced. "Did you get your bag checked yet?" he asked.

"Uh, yeah." I gestured back to the stairs with my thumb. "I handed it toward the front of the line when I was waiting." Since I had entered the doors, I heard him obnoxiously call, "Bags! Bags!" over and over. He checked each one for contraband.

"All right. You good then," he said. I proceeded forward.

"Reggie, how many times I gotta tell you? You can't bring your plants in here," the volunteer pleaded.

"Aw, come on, Bunnie. You know I'm good," Reggie jabbed.

"Oh, you all good, huh?" he mocked him.

"Yeah." Reggie snapped his fingers. I found it ironic that the volunteer's nickname was Bunnie. Reggie was the one with the large ears.

"This one time—that's all. You get another guy here checkin' and he ain't gonna be as nice." Reggie nodded coolly and rested his clenched fist in front of him. Grinning, Bunnie bumped his fist with Reggie's.

The shelter was an old, intimate rectangular hall. Two faded basketball hoops were at each end, a stage underneath one. A stereo sat on top. Funk and R&B hits from the '70s and '80s echoed off the manila-colored walls. Propped-up, heavy folding tables leaned against four wide columns that separated the general space and the wall with the kitchen. Each table had four to five old gray metal chairs. They supported both men and large bags or backpacks filled with belongings. The whole interior reminded me of the run-down facilities at the Catholic church I attended as a kid—but grimier. I wondered if the depressing off-white, orange, maroon, and yellow colors were original or if they had faded over time. The dim, suppressing yellow lighting from the high ceiling certainly didn't evoke much feeling of hope or positivity.

The shower line was a row of chairs in front of the stage. I thought to get mine out of the way before doing anything else, so I waited with my overstuffed backpack on my lap. A voice shouted the number of people needed and when those guys left, each person shuffled closer toward the end.

"I need two guys!" I heard in the near distance—my turn. I walked toward the back area of the shelter. To my left were a water fountain and an exit, and to my right was a small set of steps leading to the laundry room. A short black man named Keon stood in between two doorways, one leading to the bathroom and one leading to a room of showers. He had a squirrely vibe, like he had too much caffeine and tried to hurry to complete every task.

Rawls provided half-dollar-sized bars of ivory-colored soap, but I already had my own, as well as a travel-sized bottle of shampoo, so I only wanted a towel. I had a yoga towel but learned it worked better as a pillow. If I used my own, I'd put it in my backpack and the towel would end up smelling like a rotting animal carcass.

"I need your ticket and initials," Keon instructed. I handed him my small piece of cardboard.

"RH." He crossed my name off the list. "You need soap?"

"No. But do you have a towel?"

He dug through a laundry basket of white cloths and tossed a washcloth to me. *A washcloth?* I stared at it, biting my lip.

"You got five minutes. Starting . . . now!"

I hustled into the room. Water coated the floor. I hop-scotched my way over to the chair outside the middle shower stall. There were three. I chose the middle because its curtain was the most intact, even with tears, stains, and discoloration. I set my bag down and stripped naked, down to my now-wet flip-flops. Cautiously, I pushed the curtain aside, worried about touching the mucus-like film covering it. The shower stall itself appeared to have never been cleaned. Dark spots covered the tiled shower floor; rust colonized the showerhead; and soggy bars of soap littered the floor and the shelf protruding from the side. *We're supposed to clean ourselves in this?* I imagined catching a disease from the unsanitary condition.

"Shower two! Shower two!" Keon yelled, leaning into the doorway. *Jeez! I haven't even started washing my body.* In what seemed to be thirty-second intervals, Keon repeated the same action. "Shower two! Shower two!"

The small washcloth failed to dry my entire body. I put my dirty clothes back on, and they became instantly wet. The feel of wet cloth wrapping around my skin nauseated me. I waddled out the doorway, squeaking with each step.

We ate sauerkraut, a slice of bread, and two mushy brats for dinner. Afterward, volunteers folded the tables and slid them underneath the stage. Next, in a carefree manner, they swept and mopped the concrete-tiled floor and when dry, they dragged lavender-colored mats from a musty storage room and placed them around the room, two feet apart, starting along the wall.

Since it was my first night, I didn't know the process. By the time I learned to lean my chair against the kitchen wall while the volunteers prepped the floor, there was no room. I nervously paced back and forth, looking for a spot to sit. Guys stared at me, making my heartbeat speed up. Some of them looked hardcore—like if they weren't worried about being barred from the shelter, they'd jump me for what I had. Others looked at me curiously. I was the new guy. Instead of waiting along the wall, I decided to brush my teeth in the bathroom.

The stench thrust me back from the doorway. I couldn't recall a worse-smelling bathroom in my entire life. I inhaled deeply and bravely reentered. The cleanliness—or lack thereof—was worse than the showers. Duct tape held up the doors of two stalls, and the middle stall didn't even have a door. Gang graffiti completely covered the bathroom. The pitchfork and Playboy bunny logos were the south side gang, Gangster Disciples, and the west side gang, Vice Lords, respectively. I brushed me teeth quicker than I ever had before.

With nowhere else to sit, I sat on the small set of steps outside the laundry room, isolated from everyone else.

"Good thinking! You'll be safe there. Keep your bag next to you," a heavy white man remarked to me on his way to the bathroom. He rode in the van from Inspired Horizons. I furrowed my eyebrows in disgust. The comment belittled me. *Who was he to lecture me about safety? Why did he say it? Because I was young? Because I was in a place with rough-looking guys? Does he not think I can handle my own?* Agitation flushed through my body. When he came back, he asked my name.

"Rick," I said, avoiding eye contact.

"Rick—just don't make this your life." His soft tone and friendly eyes disarmed me, though I still didn't appreciate the idea I wasn't safe on my own. "I'm Elias." He parted his long, thick gray hair in the middle. His thick glasses scrunched together at the top of his nose. "I'm from Carbondale, down south in Illinois. I lost my job and most of the interviews that kept coming up were in Chicago, so I came up here; I thought it'd be easier if I was closer. I've been homeless for about six weeks now. I stayed in hotels the first few nights, but when I ran out of money, I looked for shelters. I slept at the Gym a couple nights, but I didn't like it."

"You like this better than the Gym?" I scoffed. "This place is a shithole—more than the Gym." In the short time I'd been at Rawls,

I'd only seen him looking paranoid, swiveling his head repeatedly and cradling his belongings.

"The bed bugs are worse there," he said.

"Oh." I sighed. It made sense. The one night I stayed there, the faded wooden floor reminded me of an old barn. It would've been a haven for bed bugs.

"Yeah." He nodded. "Where're you from, Rick?"

I told him the made-up story I used for the reason I became homeless. "Wisconsin. My mom and I don't exactly see eye to eye and one day, we got into an argument. She sort of kicked me out. I always wanted to see the city—not exactly like this—but I think around the holidays, she'll start warming up to the idea of me coming back. Until then, I'm just kind of hanging out."

"Just don't make this your life," he reemphasized.

A tall, muscular black man wearing thin-framed glasses held a clipboard with the sign-in sheet; he was the manager of Rawls. His name was Andre. He started in the corner of the room and read the names in order. Moving from each mat, which only had a thin white bedsheet on top, he dragged his feet, which I found peculiar for his body type. Andre wore a navy-blue shirt and baggy jeans. His deep, intimidating yet calming voice bellowed throughout the room. His cool presence and gap-tooth smile made me feel secure, like even though, "You gotta have balls to go Rawls," I could trust the person running it.

I ambled over to bed thirty-four. The earlier numbers lined the walls. Beds in the late twenties began inside those. I laid the single bedsheet on the disgusting thin mat and slept on top of it. The lights turned off. With nothing else to cover me, I tucked my hands inside my hoodie sleeves and hoped for a peaceful night.

"Don't let the bed bugs bite!" someone yelled. The room of sixty-plus guys filled with laughter.

"Oh, they gon' bite!" another guy shouted. Roars of louder laughter shook the shelter walls. My dimples hurt from smiling. It was the funniest thing I heard in a month. Before it, the only jokes were inside my head.

CHAPTER FOUR

I'M ALREADY IN IT

"Farouk, you comin'?" Phil yelled out the passenger window, leaning over Reggie. We had just begun our ride to Rawls, but we stopped at the end of the alleyway. A short man froze on the sidewalk. He wore an oversized blue coat and a puzzled face. "I said, 'Are you comin', Farouk?'" The man wobbled back and forth, hesitating to decide. Phil shook his head. "Just get in."

Farouk hopped in the van and squeezed next to me. "What's your name?" he asked me in a high-pitched, prepubescent voice. The concept of personal space evaded him; he leaned toward me, a couple inches from my face. I'd never met anyone so comfortable cozying up to a complete stranger. I noticed a small, discolored patch on his neck. I wouldn't have noticed it if we weren't so close together.

"Rick," I answered, subtly tilting my head away from his. His breath smelled ashy. He probably hadn't brushed his teeth for some time, either.

"I'm Farouk," he said, smiling wide. "Where're you from?"

"Wisconsin," I replied. A wrinkle formed in his large forehead.

He didn't know where it was. "Well, so if we're in Chicago, Wisconsin is like an hour north." His wrinkle grew larger.

Reggie barged into our conversation. "Oh, he don't know where that is. He probably don't even know we're in Chicago. All he knows is Kenya—or whatever country he's from," Reggie teased. "What country you from again?"

Farouk laughed. "Nigeria!" I tried to remember where Nigeria was on a map of Africa. I could've sworn it was somewhere on the west side of the large continent.

Phil whipped his head around. "Farouk, you ain't steppin' on my bag, are you? I got my weed in there!" Farouk giggled and moved his feet away from a small blue duffle bag. "You don't believe me? When we get out, we gonna smoke it." Farouk smiled, open-mouthed. Phil turned to the passenger seat. "Reggie, you want in?"

"Hell yeah! I roll some real nice blunts," Reggie announced.

Phil turned back to Farouk. "See, there you go. Reggie is down." Reggie and Phil seemed tight.

"Phil, Farouk was downtown begging today. Can you see Farouk begging?" Reggie altered his voice to a high pitch. "'Hi, could you spot me three dollars?'" He clapped his hands with a loud smack.

Everyone in the van laughed. Reggie then slapped the dashboard, laughing.

"Boy, can you see that?" Reggie cracked me up. So far, he was the most entertaining person I had met—not just since I became homeless, but in my life. He was like an outrageous character I'd only watched on TV.

Another guy said, "Farouk, you'd make more money putting out a Michael Jackson record. You sound just like him."

"I want to rock with you . . ." Reggie sang, snapping his fingers.

Farouk sighed. "Guys . . ."

"Farouk, why you talkin'? You ain't got no weed in you yet," Phil teased.

"But seriously, Farouk," Reggie started, "if you need money, let one of us know. You don't need to do that." Farouk didn't hear him, or maybe he intentionally ignored him so he could continue begging in the future.

Throughout the remainder of the ride, Farouk dozed off and rested his head on my shoulder. I didn't say anything. It was obvious he was well liked and as a rather-new guy, I didn't think I had built up the clout to confront him. Farouk had a naïvety, a carefreeness about him and a willingness to laugh. He was adorable—lovable, even. Luckily, whenever Phil turned onto another street, Farouk slid off me.

I finished my quick shower and sat at a table. I found it better to get it out of the way immediately, especially because the line was shorter earlier in the night. Upbeat songs played from the stereo on stage. "Ring My Bell" filled the room. I read the *Chicago Reader*, a free weekly newspaper known for their literary pieces on politics, art, and food. It provided more reading content to *kill* time and, unlike the free daily newspaper, *Chicago Red Eye*, it wasn't completely saturated with ads and one-paragraph articles. It was meant to be read, not scanned during a commute.

"That's by us, you know," a deep voice said. I looked up. Marquis caught me off guard. He was a large black man with thick-lensed glasses, also part of the Inspired Horizons program. I saw him and Reggie together a lot. Marquis's soft, teddy-bear-like demeanor meshed well with Reggie's over-the-top personality.

My newspaper was open to the cover story, "Criminal Courts." The centerfold included photos of three basketball courts in separate neighborhoods. "In the name of protecting kids, there's a movement to take away their sports equipment."

Marquis said, "The Alderman removed the rims from a park near us at Horizons. Gang activity is up, and people feel gangs can recruit members on the courts and do drug deals. In the past week, there've been two shootings—one of which killed a two-year-old from a stray bullet."

"Dang. Really?" I asked with wide eyes, pushing up my glasses. It seemed like a dumb idea to me. That was the best idea people came up with to curb gang activity? In college, every now and then, I'd shoot hoops outside but grew frustrated with the limited options. I'd argue that more basketball hoops should be erected.

He nodded. "Gangs hang out by the red line stop. They sell drugs and when rivals walk by, they shoot down from the windows above. That's why I always take the Broadway exit on the Wilson stop instead of the Wilson exit." Marquis wasn't the first person who mentioned that, which is why I, too, exited onto Broadway. A police SUV always parked underneath the L stop. I already witnessed several arrests. "One day, I was doing laundry and there were shootings in the parking lot. Two people were shot and there was blood all over." He paused. "Are you ready for all this?" he asked.

"I'm already in it," I said. He nodded. I was well aware of my surroundings—probably too aware for my own good. I teetered between hyperaware and paranoid.

A shirtless man stormed out of the shower area on the opposite side of the room from Marquis and me. "This is the worst shelter I've been at!" he shouted. "I'm not staying at this shithole!"

Marquis and I looked at each other.

The man marched to his backpack at the table adjacent to us and stuffed it with the rest of his belongings. He pulled the zipper so aggressively that it caught the threads. "Ah shit!" he yelled. Red marks and lacerations covered his entire upper body. I wondered if he had a skin disease or if someone had attacked him.

"What happened to your back?" Marquis asked. I thought it was brash to ask the man how he got the marks, but Marquis's soft voice cushioned his inquiry.

"Bed bugs bit me like crazy at the last shelter—and now this!" He shook his head and threw his backpack around his shoulder, rushed to the exit, and stomped up the steps.

I asked Marquis, "You think it was something specific or just everything here?"

"I don't know. Not everyone can handle Rawls."

At the end of the table, Farouk sat unfazed. He never looked up. His large yellow eyes concentrated on pouring a can of orange soda into a two-liter bottle of Hawaiian Punch. He spilled it several times and giggled at his sticky hands. Nothing seemed to stress Farouk. I wished I had a threshold like him.

I turned back to Marquis.

"I know it's a dump, but from your experience, is Rawls a safe place to stay?"

He shrugged. "It's all right. Make sure you're alert and know what's going on. Keep an eye on your stuff too."

"Yeah, tell me about it." I rolled my eyes. "Someone already stole my watch."

He shook his head at the floor. "How'd that happen?"

"It was back on my first night here," I said. "You know, sometimes I wake up and just like to check the time to see how much longer I can sleep. So I dug through my backpack for my watch. It was only five twenty, and guys told me the night before that the lights came on at five forty-five, so I thought I had another twenty-five minutes. I put it right next to my face so I could read it still lying down. I dozed off, and it was gone when the lights turned on."

Marquis sighed and shook his head.

"And then get this. Two days later in the dayroom, I saw that munchkin-lookin' dude wearing it."

"That guy who always tries to sell people shit?"

"Yeah, the guy who brags that he gets everything from the five-finger discount."

"I think his name is Darren," Marquis said.

I relaxed my shoulders. "Well, at least now I won't be stupid and leave my stuff out." It angered me that someone stole things from other homeless individuals. But I didn't think that concept registered to him. He saw something possibly valuable and grabbed it. If someone truly needed that item, they probably shouldn't have been so neglectful.

Guys began shuffling into the dinner line. Neither Marquis nor I were in a hurry. We continued our conversation.

Marquis said, "The only reason I like going to Rawls better than the Gym is because you know those wood floors over there have more bed bugs." Those red marks on that guy's back flashed in my mind. "Showers aren't mandatory there, either. I'm not comfortable with that. At least I know everyone here will be clean," he said. "The people here are rougher, though. You gotta watch yourself. You might get a little flack 'cause you're white—maybe verbal arguments—but it probably won't escalate into violence. Some people are prejudiced here. Some blacks don't like the whites, and some whites don't like the blacks. It's dumb, but that's the way some people are."

"Mhm." It baffled me. But I also understood I was younger than everyone in the shelter—intense racial contentiousness was something I never experienced. "I basically just mind my business and, if people are friendly enough, I wouldn't mind having some conversations—like us right now."

"Yeah, that's good." Marquis pointed to a young black guy people referred to as Biggie. "You see that guy over there?" His pants hung below his butt, exposing his royal-blue smiley-faced boxers. He talked to himself as if there was another person. He tapped his hands on tables constantly, making beats and rapping lyrics he had just written in his notebook. Andre told him to stop several times— even once when the lights were off. "He was in jail with me. No one thought he was all the way there—mentally, you know?"

"Uh huh." I slid to the edge of my seat and put one elbow on the table.

"He irritated the hell out of everyone by doing that tapping, but he never messed with anyone, so no one ever did anything about it. If you don't get into other people's business, you should be fine."

"Makes sense." I quickly glanced around the room. Generic soda cans and empty bags of chips on the table replaced the men who waited in the dinner line.

"I'm forty-six. Do you think I want to start shit and everything? No. We're all in here for one reason or another. The way I see it, we all need each other for support. No one should have to live like this." He waved his hands around the room. "Yeah, you can tell people have different education levels, but we're all here, trying to manage."

Marquis didn't have a high-level education, but he was wise. His demeanor was calm and reflective. He learned from his mistakes, and it shaped his perspective.

"I used to get high all the time with my friends. But luckily, I had family up here till about two years ago. They convinced me to stop," he emphasized. "Got sober for about a year and a half, but then I left my job for a new one that paid more. I'd work on a Sunday and walk away with five hundred dollars at night. I was making more money than ever, and I didn't know what to do with it. I got back into drugs," he confessed, "but stopping was the smartest thing I've ever done. We all have our reasons for being here, and each person has a different story—but you know what? We're all here."

"True." Everyone in the room was equal; everyone was homeless.

"I started a relationship with God. I'd been avoiding him for most of my life. I thought I had all the answers and didn't need to listen to anyone," he admitted. "People wanted to help me, but I pushed them away. Pretty soon, though, everyone left. That was scary. I fell. Humbled, man." He swatted the air. "What'd I have to lose by praying to God?"

His body mirrored his story. He slugged his body around with an exhaustion far surpassing an average forty-six-year-old. Life had already worn him down. His buzz-cut hairstyle symbolized he had enough. He wanted a change, an acceptance of a different, simple kind of life.

Reggie strolled over to our table, dancing to "Le Freak" blaring from the stereo.

"Marquis! Slick Rick! Show me what you got," he cheered, snapping his fingers. I smiled from ear to ear. It was the first time I had been called Slick Rick. I never had a nickname—at least one that stuck. When I was younger, my older sister's friends called me Dimples and Smiles. In high school, my friend dubbed me JV Superstar, due to my athletic prowess peaking at age fifteen. But nothing cool like Slick Rick.

Marquis chuckled but remained sitting.

I waved off Reggie. "I'm good, man. I can't dance."

"That ain't good enough." He lifted me from my seat. "Come on, now."

Soon, I shifted my bodyweight, moved my arms as if an electric current flowed through it, and glided in a circle, giving the appearance of floating.

"Whew-ee! That ain't bad! Where'd you learn that?"

"Usher." I had a mild obsession in high school with learning how to dance like him.

"Mhm. That brother can dance. What else you got?"

"That's about all I got." I laughed harder than before, clutching my stomach. I had about three dance moves in my repertoire. "I'm not as smooth as you, Reggie Ice-Cold Tellers."

"Oh, snap!" Reggie snorted and clapped me on the back. He dashed to several tables. "Guys! You gotta hear what my guy, Slick Rick, came up with for me! He called me Reggie *Ice-Cold* Tellers! Ain't that a sweet name?"

Had I known Reggie would actually take it to heart, I would've come up with something more creative. I just ripped it from the DJ on V103, the radio station we listened to in the van. Either way, Reggie liked it.

Marquis heaved himself from his chair, and we made our way into the dinner line.

With a toothbrush in one hand and toothpaste in the other, I walked through the bathroom doorway. A stocky man of average height, pointed nose, and countless freckles on his face stood in front of the mirror, applying shaving cream to his five o' clock shadow.

"You mind if I use the other sink?" I asked.

"No, go ahead," he said.

His name was Vinny, and he already reminded me of a stereotypical Chicago guy. He was a blue-collar-type, with a slight Chicago accent. His navy-blue Bears shirt was probably one of eight he owned.

He slid the razor across his face and turned to me. "Gentlemen are always clean-cut," he said. He couldn't keep his eye off my beard. "Plus, it helps in interviews."

I rubbed my hairy chin. "Well, I guess I'm not a gentleman."

He changed the topic. "I don't want to be here. Once I get enough money, my dad and I are outta here."

I nodded, my toothbrush still hanging from my mouth as I turned on the water. I finished brushing my teeth, and my momentum pulled me toward the door.

"It was nice meeting you," I said. "I'll see you around." *Did he say his dad was here too?* I thought. *He'd have to be in his sixties or seventies. How'd that happen? What a peculiar situation.*

Journal Entry — September 13, 2011

I'm going to keep staying at Rawls for a while. Before, I worried that people inside the shelter would look at me inquisitively, but that hasn't been the case. Many know my general story: that I'm from Wisconsin and don't really get along with my mom. That's all I've needed to really share. Guys get it. We all have issues and reasons for being here. Let's get through it together, like Marquis said. It first really hit me when I filled out the intake form with the Department of Human Services. The woman marked me as *in-transit*. Domestic abuse, fleeing gang violence, family issues, loss of job, traveling, and substance abuse were other listed reasons. I also learned that some people, mainly youth, become homeless because they're gay and their families don't accept them.

I notice some people are adamant about not being in this position long—almost like being homeless is an insult to them. Without bringing it up in conversation, they vehemently deny the label of *homeless*. It's like they're aware of the ideas and images of *homeless* ingrained within society but feel they don't fit under it. It's like they're not only trying to battle their individual situation of being homeless, but also the burden of being swept under the category of *the homeless*.

It seems like a lot of guys—at Rawls especially—have been homeless before. Not many are the stereotypical homeless. They aren't totally messed up mentally or out begging on the streets. Yesterday, during the van ride, Reggie pointed to a man sitting on a bench with his head down, surrounded by bags. He said, "Damn. No one should have to live like that." I thought it was interesting.

I act like myself for the most part, but tone down my smiling and enthusiasm. I swear more than usual, but not too much. Most of the guys are much older than me—in their thirties, forties, and fifties. When I tell them I'm twenty-two, they immediately begin encouraging me that there's so much more to life. It's inspiring.

Guys know they made mistakes—that's why they're here. They express regret burning bridges and relationships. They're alone now and don't have many who care about them. They don't have someone to pass their wisdom to. Maybe it's natural they gravitate toward someone young like me. I just listen and ask questions.

Every day, there's so much information to soak up. It's tough to document it all, but I do the best I can. I don't feel comfortable whipping out my memo pad and writing down everything that happens in the moment. I'm not interested in being a journalist getting quotes, although I do remember them. I scribble down notes in the dark when we're all in bed.

Living homeless has become more structured, so I can't go all around the city like my first month. I have to be at Inspired Horizons by 4:45

p.m. every day, making my free time 6:00 a.m. to 3:30 p.m. I go to breakfast, but after that, I spend time typing my journals. I go to the Loyola Information Commons. I use my driver's license to get a guest pass. After getting a computer code, I can basically stay until midnight. At first, I used the Chicago Public Library computers, but access is limited to two hours. It's too short—plus the keyboards are always crusty and tough to type on. I still kill time at the Chicago libraries though, especially the Harold Washington one downtown.

Staying in the shelter reminds me of a summer camp: a large group of people following lots of structure and rules. I don't mind it *too* much right now. I sleep better than in the parks. A lot of guys hate it and knock it, especially guys staying their first night. It's a shithole—that's obvious. They're shocked by the appalling conditions. They wonder *aloud* how a place like Rawls is allowed to exist. I've heard numerous guys, at both Inspired Horizons and Rawls, question if their dignity is being violated.

CHAPTER FIVE

FACES ON THE INTERNET

It was 6:45 in the evening. We waited outside Rawls. The locked shelter doors looked more intimidating than a medieval castle; the shelter was impenetrable until seven, leaving us to kill time on the sidewalk outside. Some guys walked to the gas station a quarter mile away to buy soda and squares, a new term I learned meant cigarettes.

"Where do you go during the day?" Elias asked me, pulling a drag from his "square."

"Well, I spend most of my time at the libraries. I go on the computers and read books," I explained. "I figured since I have some time, I ought to go back and reread some of the books I was supposed to in high school. You know, those classics like F. Scott Fitzgerald and stuff. Grades were emphasized in school—not learning—so I used to just go to SparkNotes and study that way. I guess I'm trying to catch up now."

"That's all right." A puff of smoke escaped his mouth. "You're maturing, and you're not fully baked until your thirties."

I chuckled. "How're things going for you? How long do you

figure you'll be here?" I asked, pulling my sweatshirt sleeves lower. The cool air had suddenly become cooler.

"I don't put a number on it because I hear other people say they're leaving this day or that day, and they're still here when the date arrives. I don't want to do that."

I nodded. "That's a good idea."

"Do as much as you can and let time run its course." He smashed the cigarette into the ground. Elias traveled all over the city each day, working hard to find a job and housing. "I'm going to a résumé workshop and networking event next week. You can join too, if you'd like, Rick."

"Thanks, Elias."

The older Dominican man standing next to us joined our conversation. His name was Juan. I saw him before at Rawls. His skin was dark. He wore a blue baseball cap on his bald head. He was handsome, with brilliant green eyes and long eyelashes.

"I met a woman on a bus, today," Juan said, standing on a patch of weeds growing from the sidewalk crack. "She's forty and married, but apparently the marriage isn't working out too well. She gave me her son's cell phone number instead of her home phone. You know, normally, I wouldn't hit on a married woman . . . but I'm desperate." He laughed. Elias and I smiled until Juan's face turned serious, like a professor about to deliver the key to life to his students. "People underestimate marriages. They think it will be easy, but they learn it's not. They need to communicate better—you're dealing with a human being and sometimes people change. The goal is to change together for the better." He gestured with his hand. "You know, it's sad a lot of marriages don't work out."

"You seem to have a lot of wisdom about marriages," I said.

A smile broke across his face. "I've been married four times." We burst into laughter. "Get this—one time, I was married to a Korean woman and then after we split, I married her sister!"

Elias and I shook our heads and grinned.

From the corner of my eye, I spotted Vinny marching toward us. He bombarded our triangle. "You still haven't shaved yet, huh?" he blabbered. He squinted his eyes and pointed to patchy areas in my beard. "You got some wild areas there. You're not a bad-lookin' guy. I bet if you got rid of it, you'd get a ton more girls. I mean, I'm not gay or anything or homophobic." He waved his hands. "A survey was done online and like four hundred thousand girls answered it. Only four percent said they liked guys with beards—and only two percent said they liked guys with beards *and* glasses."

"Oh yeah? What's the source of the survey?" I asked, quizzing the accuracy of his facts.

"The website of one of those girly magazines," he proclaimed. He flicked his wrist. "I'll bring you a razor tomorrow, and you can shave it. I want to see what you look like."

"Nah, that's all right. I'm not shaving it."

Vinny clenched his jaw. He turned to his left. "Hey, stupid!" Vinny called toward an old, confused-looking man. "Get over here, Dad. Don't be an idiot and walk away!"

Elias, Juan, and I locked eyes at each other. *Did he really call his own father stupid and an idiot?*

Vinny attached his hands to his father's shoulders, guiding him toward us. He was short with a few white hairs on his head, which made his dark-brown eyebrows stand out. For his age, I was surprised he didn't wear glasses. His thinness looked unhealthy. "He's had two strokes," Vinny informed us. "The doctor says he has the brain of a ten-year-old." The man gazed around us like a spacey spirit.

"Me and my dad have walked over three hundred and eighty-five miles since coming here to Rawls. We walked to Navy Pier, Wrigley Field—you name it, and we've probably walked there," he boasted. "Did you know the top five exercises you can do are jogging, swimming, biking, walking, and sex?" He placed his bag on the ground. "I'll demonstrate for you guys." He paced forward ten feet. He waddled like how I imagined a Neanderthal would. Juan, Elias, and I looked at each other again. We all rolled our eyes, snickering.

Vinny scolding his father made me uncomfortable. Caring for an ill father, especially while homeless, must have been difficult, but shepherding him around like an animal seemed abusive. I didn't want other guys to affiliate me with the behavior, so I tried to distance myself from him.

───────

Reggie and I waited in the shower line together. The stereo on the stage behind us wasn't playing any music. I wondered why. The silence made the vibe more tense.

"Someone stole my bag! Someone stole my bag!" a man yelled, rushing from the shower area. Reggie and I turned our heads. "Someone stole my bag!" The man marched past us and into Andre's office, along the kitchen wall.

I ran my hand through my longer-than-usual hair. *Jeez. This stuff is happening all the time.* What baffled me more was that hardly anyone reacted to it. It was normal. Reggie didn't say anything—he watched the room like me.

After a few minutes, Andre and the man emerged from the office. Andre walked thirty feet to the center of the room. His voice boomed, "I've been nice to you guys so far, but this shit can't be goin' on! Y'all can't be takin' stuff that don't belong to ya. I don't want to burn y'all, but if I have to, I'm gonna burn each and every one of ya."

Reggie nudged me. "That's why you keep to yourself. There's criminals in here. There are murderers and sexual offenders and shit."

I gulped. "You serious?"

"Yeah. If you go on the internet, you're gonna see a lot of these faces." He scanned the room with his pointed finger. I bit my lip. "The pedophiles and child molesters are the worst kind, man. Their heads aren't right. You don't know what they're gonna do. Make sure you keep to yourself, man—especially since you a white boy."

"Oh. Uh, okay." I squirmed. A sudden light-headedness came over me. I took a deep breath. Reggie nudged me again.

"You okay, Rick? You look like you about to fall over. This ain't no joke, man."

"Look." I pointed. A man with a shaved head and tattoos followed Andre into his office. "That must be the guy who stole the bag. He must've admitted or got caught."

"No one admits, Rick. Someone ratted. Whad'ya know—thief's a skinhead!" Reggie shrieked.

Reggie's comments sobered me up quickly. Until then, I had started getting used to Rawls and Inspired Horizons. My loneliness had receded gradually, but I found myself on edge again, like my first night. *What would happen to me if I let my guard down again? Something worse than my backpack being stolen? Guys don't say, "You gotta have balls to go to Rawls," for no reason.*

CHAPTER SIX

VINNY'S PROPOSITION

Originally from Europe, George spent his last few days at Rawls. Guys believed methadone—a drug used to treat the addiction of heroin—caused his mumbled tangents and outbursts of laughter. His wife stayed at the overnight women's shelter affiliated with Inspired Horizons.

Phil turned to the tightly packed group of men in the van. "Wait. Who's that guy who has that TV show?" He snapped his fingers, trying to remember. "He sings 'Crazy Train.'"

"Ozzy Osbourne!" Reggie shouted from the passenger seat.

Phil pointed to George. "Yeah, you're Ozzy!"

Everyone laughed at the doppelganger suggestion, including George. It was spot-on—the voice, hair, and spacey behavior. Surprisingly though, he had a good memory. One night at Rawls, someone walked around selling cans of soda for fifty cents. I didn't drink soda much, but for whatever reason had a hankering for something sweet. I bought a Sprite, and Ozzy asked if I could spot him. I didn't think much of it. I had a handful of loose change in my backpack. Two days later, he approached me in the dayroom at Inspired Horizons and handed me a bottle of Sprite to repay me.

Phil continued on a serious note. "We have more people coming every day now so the numbers are finna go up since it's cold. It's different than the summer. My company told me to relay it to you. What you need to do is show up because, otherwise, the city is gonna think they don't need to pay for certain things if the numbers aren't there. I'm tryin' to help y'all."

Traffic was slow on Ashland. We tended to hit the tail end of rush hour. The red light backed up cars for a half mile. Phil turned around while we sat.

"You guys got it good right now—freedom, free meals during the day, and a place to stay at night."

"Bullshit! You don't want to be us," Reggie shot from the passenger seat.

Phil swung his head back around. "I'll trade places with you. No problem!"

"Well, when you do, I'mma take your girl, Phil," Reggie jabbed back.

"Fine! Everyone's suckin' all the money out of me anyway. Every time she shows me her tits, I have to pay for something. I barely got enough money for food. It sucks. I make a bologna sandwich and go in the next room and when I come back, the kid takes it—it's gone. At least when you make a sandwich, it's still there or you can put it away. I mean damn, it's a Saturday and I just wanna watch a movie and have a drink, but I can't 'cause I gotta pick up y'all asses." He raised his shoulders, catching his breath.

"You whine like a little bitch!" Reggie hissed.

Phil threw his arm in the air. The red light turned to green, and we continued south on Ashland.

The interactions between Phil and Reggie cracked me up. They made any subject matter funny. Their banter had such chemistry, as if they'd grown up together. I could only imagine the mischief they'd find themselves in if they starred in a body-swap sitcom.

Phil looked up at the rearview mirror. "Where you from?" he asked a black man sitting on my bench. "I haven't seen you before."

"Ghana," he replied. His black skin was darker than everyone's except Farouk's. But unlike Farouk, he was still learning American humor and culture. It took longer for him to sort through conversations. He even sat differently than others, with a straightened back, clutching his backpack placed perfectly symmetrical on his thighs. The rest of us leaned back and handled our backpack with little care. Of anything, his casual blue jeans and T-shirt helped him blend in the most.

"Ghana? Shit, man," Phil said. "What's your name?"

"Dodzi."

"Dodzi?" Phil muttered back to himself. He smiled and shook his head.

"You're from Africa too?" Farouk asked.

"Yes. What do you do?" Dodzi asked Farouk.

"Farouk doesn't do anything," Phil butted in. "He just smokes reefer."

Farouk raised his voice. "Hey, why are you trying to embarrass me?"

Phil ignored Farouk and spoke straight to Dodzi. "What do you want to do?"

He thought for a moment and said, "I want to get a job."

"What do you do?" Phil asked.

Dodzi shrugged. "Anything."

"*Anything?* You have to be more specific and know what you want," Phil said. "So if I give a pair of boots to you right now and tell you to clean the sewers and pay you five dollars an hour, you're going to do it? Because that's a job." The man furrowed his eyebrows. "What do you do?" Phil repeated.

He remained quiet. The rest of the guys in the van stared at him, awaiting his response. His eyes wandered from the uncomfortable attention, but Phil broke the silence.

"What skills do you have?"

"None." He paused again. His eyes looked to the van roof. "Restaurant or general labor," he answered.

"Now we're getting somewhere!" Phil threw his hands in the air and a smile stretched across his face.

Dodzi said, "I want to work for a bit to make some money and then go to Truman College to get an education."

"All right! Well, just stay away from this guy." He pointed to Farouk with a teasing smile.

Farouk laughed. "Hey!"

Phil cared deeply for the well-being of the men. He jabbed and badgered guys, but that was his personality. Numerous times along our route to Rawls, he parked in front of buildings, explaining the organization's resources and how it could benefit them. He warned us to stay consistent using resources and services, or else funding would disappear. One time, a veteran left his phone in the dayroom and Phil turned the van around to help him out. He said, "I'm only doing this 'cause you're a veteran." Deep down, I knew he'd do it for others too. It was his nature to help others. He'd also say, "I can show you all these places, but at the end of the day, I can't go to work for y'all."

———

I refilled my silver water bottle at the dented water fountain. For as run-down as Rawls was, its water was somehow the best I ever drank. It was always cold.

A voice confronted me. "Hey, Rick!" Vinny stood a few feet away. I had been trying to distance myself from him, but he was persistent. Almost every night, immediately as I signed in, he waved his arms at me, calling my name from across the room. "Rick! Sit here! I saved a spot for you."

At a place where I saw the same people every day, there was only so much I could do to avoid Vinny without it being awkward. It wasn't so much the clinginess that bothered me—it was the irritating comments. He lacked self-awareness. He often spoke out of turn and suffocated conversations by talking over others. He never failed to seize the moment to get the last word in. His personality disallowed others to be the focus. And God knows Vinny was never wrong.

So when Vinny cornered me, I couldn't help but brace myself

for another annoying interaction—probably about how I needed to shave my beard.

"I have a proposition for you." I prepared for offered compensation for shaving my face. "I'm only helping two people out, and you're the second," he said. "I know someone who could get you in as a city of Chicago worker. They're looking for young people to work there twenty-five to thirty years and then retire."

My mouth fell open. "Uh. Um. Well, I—"

He continued without giving me a chance to respond. "You get paid thirty-two dollars an hour and get a great pension. New York City workers only get paid eighteen dollars an hour—and in LA, they make only eleven dollars an hour. My dad used to come home with three-thousand-dollar checks."

"Wow. That's a lot. I've never made that much money." Now I knew why Illinois had such terrible financial problems.

"I know. Chicago is the greatest city in the Midwest—everything has to come through here. You could live well in the city. I'll talk to the guy again tomorrow." He flicked his wrist at me. "Once me and my dad get a place, I'll let you stay with me until you find something—get back on your feet and make some money."

I stood still. I never imagined someone would offer me housing *and* a job. I leaned back and forth with my hands in my pockets, pausing to collect my thoughts. I didn't want to waste his time helping me with something I didn't want (or technically need). I appreciated his willingness, which probably stemmed from his proclaimed religiousness, but I dug my heels deeper into my reason for experiencing homeless.

"I don't know, Vinny. Right now is not the right time. Eventually, I would like to go back to Wisconsin and be by my family when everything works out." He pinched his lips; his nostrils flared as his breathing grew heavier. He teased me before that twenty-two-year-olds were naïve and immature, but here, I acted like it. He grinded his teeth to convince me to accept his help.

"You'd only be ninety miles away from your family. My family is all the way over in Croatia. This is a great job."

"I know. I know." I stared at the dark spots on the ground. "I just can't right now," I squeaked out. "I'm sorry. Thank you, though." His focused eyes turned teary. His arms limped at his side. It looked like I had just kicked his puppy.

The whole situation made me feel uneasy. I thought of Dodzi. He was determined to get a job, to make money to put toward an education that would improve his life. And Phil's advice was valuable: know what you want, know what you're good at, be prepared, and take the path that will take you where you want to go. I found it refreshing. Most people probably viewed homeless individuals as desperate, willing to take any job. Phil advised against it. *Why should a homeless person's career path or hopes be any different than someone with a home?* I thought.

Dodzi actively sought a job and instead, I was offered a good job. It wasn't because I had skills—it was because Vinny liked me enough to help. I felt shameful, being caught in the crossfire of a scenario that played out *too* often within society. Success often came down to who you know. Most Americans wanted to believe we lived in a meritocracy, where the selection of positions was based on the ability of each individual. To a point, yes. But then why in college did the term *networking* become such a big deal? I didn't like it. As a first-generation college student who grew up on a farm, I witnessed the connections my peers' parents had in the city. It made me feel behind and insignificant at times.

And now I watched it happen in the homeless shelter.

CHAPTER SEVEN

NEW FACES

I walked away from the kitchen with a full plate in my hand. Reggie sat at a table, sedate stillness replacing his over-the-top mannerisms. I'd seen him become hot and cold before, but not prolonged. One of those times, he muttered to me, "We're not living—we're just existing." Something troubling stirred inside him. The van ride to Rawls was uneventful without his energy. I tried joking with him twice before leaving him be.

A tall man wearing a black Oakland Raiders Starter jacket swiveled his head, looking for a place to eat his dinner.

"You can sit with me, man," I said, waving him over.

"Thanks."

I guided him toward my table, parallel to the wall. We sat down across from each other. His name was Max. He was Peruvian but originally from New York. "So what do you do?" I asked. I stuck my fork into the canned olive-colored green beans.

"I work at a place near O'Hare, answering phone calls," he said.

"Phone calls for what?" I asked, chewing the leathery beans in my mouth.

"Specialized colleges and infomercials."

"Wait. What? You mean like those ads on TV late at night?"

His black bowl-cut-shaped hair danced as he chuckled. "Yeah."

"What's that like?" My eager interest caught him off guard.

He swallowed his spaghetti. "Uh, I don't mind it. It isn't very boring because the phones ring quite a bit."

"Really?" I leaned closer to him. "I never thought people actually called." I continued eating my beans.

"Yeah, a lot of times people call drunk or stoned. That makes it more entertaining."

"What were the most interesting calls you received?" I asked.

He paused to think. He then pulled his jacket over his head. He set it on the chair with his backpack. "Ah. That's better." He wiped the sweat from his brow. "A woman called about returning to school for her master's degree. I asked her when she last graduated and heard ninety-one, so I didn't think anything of it. I was surprised by how soft her voice was"—he squinted his brown eyes—"turns out she was ninety-one *years* old, not graduated from high school in ninety-one."

I jerked my head back, my eyes bulging. "Whoa! Sounds like a pretty ambitious woman."

He cracked a smile. "Yeah, I know, right?"

I looked toward the ceiling. There was a constant clicking noise that irritated me. A thick rope was usually tied to the side of the wall. It was loose and the ceiling fan kept hitting it. I peered around the room to see if anyone else noticed it. Apparently, the loud noise wasn't a big deal to anyone else.

"I live far from the job and want to move closer. It typically takes me five hours to get to and from work each day," Max said.

"Five hours? Dang! That's a long time." I couldn't blame him. I couldn't ever do that. I'd get antsy with anything over an hour-long, one-way commute. I put a forkful of noodles in my mouth. It was overly seasoned to conceal its blandness.

"Yeah." He nodded. "I looked at a few places, but they all rented right away. I tried getting help from an apartment agency, and they told me I had two evictions—evictions for places I never even lived at!" His face burnt red. "I took a week off of work to figure things out. But right now, I'm homeless."

I shook my head. "Oh my God, man. I'm sorry to hear that."

"Thanks." He frowned. "What I really should do is move somewhere else, like I have in the past—get out of this Midwest weather."

"Yeah? Have you lived anywhere else before?"

He cleared his plate, and he swallowed his last bite. "Mhm. South America, Europe, and other parts of the US. I loved Seattle. The aura there is awesome. The whole Pacific Northwest is neat because everybody minds their own business and lives carefree."

"Doesn't it rain all the time there?" I asked.

"Yeah, but that's what makes it cool too."

I laughed. "What? How can that be?"

He smiled. "I told you—it's that aura."

"What about Europe? Where'd you live there?"

"Denmark and Holland. I was in Holland on September eleventh. My boss sent me home from work early. He worried about my safety because of my dark skin—people in Holland have prejudices. They wouldn't care if I'm Hispanic—only that I'm brown," he said. "That shook me for a while. That's when I decided to come back to America."

"Damn." I shook my head. My 9/11 experience was much different. I was in literature class in seventh grade. My teacher informed us of what happened, but I didn't even know what a terrorist attack was. The remainder of the day, I was glued to computers and televisions. But Max was on the other side of the world. He had to be concerned about what other people thought of him. He was in danger solely because of the color of his skin. And he wanted to return to America because he believed he'd be more accepted for who he was. My mind worked harder to process that. I always heard criticisms of race in America. I'd been conditioned to automatically think negatively about the country's relationship with race. Max brought up a new perspective.

"Rick, you missed the coffee yesterday morning," Elias informed me.

"Oh, Rawls had coffee?" Juan snapped his fingers. "I missed it too."

"Don't worry"—Elias flipped his hand—"it's nothing special. It's just generic instant coffee, even the coffee at Horizons breakfast is better."

"That's a pretty bold statement," I remarked. I looked up to the opposite corner of the room. The fan still kept hitting the rope. It drove me batty that no one had fixed it yet.

A stumpy man wearing a White Sox shirt butted in. It was Darren. "You guys need coffee? I'll sell you this Dunkin' Donuts gift card. Forty-two dollars on it for twenty."

Elias and Juan rolled their eyes. "Nah, we don't need it," I said.

"First come, first serve. You're missing out." He went about his business, asking others if they wanted to buy candy he got from the convenience store down the street.

"That's the guy who stole my watch," I sneered to Elias and Juan. "I told Marquis about him the other day."

"How do you know that?" Elias asked. Darren wasn't wearing the watch at the time.

"I lost it the first night I stayed here. He was here too. Two days later, I saw him wearing it in the dayroom—identical to mine. People don't go watch-shopping and choose to buy that one. It's cheap and ugly. It's bright white and snaps onto your wrist. You can't even adjust the time on it. You have to find the real time, compare it to the watch, and then do the math each time. I never even wore it. I just pulled it from my backpack to check the time. I didn't say anything to him. I didn't want to start something. But it's too coincidental. It only cost six dollars at Walgreens, but it's more so the principle, you know?" I noticed it when he went around trying to sell a stolen portable CD player to others. I sat at a table against the mural wall and grinded my teeth the whole time.

Juan leaned in to us, lowering his voice. "I overheard from a few guys that he has some money and flaunts it. People don't like him." He nudged Elias. "He even told me he has six hundred dollars and then showed me a stack of lottery tickets and gift cards."

Our conversation halted when a guy yelled, "Someone stole my phone!" We all turned our heads to Darren. He darted toward us to check his backpack.

I smirked as I watched him rummage through his brand-new brown backpack. Others openly laughed at him. People called him a dumbass for leaving it out. Darren's face turned sour from holding back tears. He tasted his own medicine and didn't like it. I couldn't remember another moment when I wished ill will on someone—but I did that day.

Does that make me a bad person? Karma just winked at me and, somehow, it feels a little dirty.

I moved too slowly again and missed my chance to sit along the wall. I sat on the small set of steps again. At least the ceiling noise was suppressed where I was. A pudgy man spoke to Keon.

"Metallica, Black Sabbath, Iron Maiden. I love metal." I saw the man earlier talking to the parole officer at the shelter entrance.

"You like Black Sabbath?" I asked, pointing to the showers. "That was Ozzy who just went into the showers."

Keon widened his eyes, and the other man laughed.

"Yeah, man. That guy's messed up. He probably did more drugs than Ozzy—probably soaked them in acid too."

The Puerto Rican man's name was Armando. He had long, curly hair that he tied in a ponytail. Two teardrop tattoos floated below his eyes on his acne-scarred face. His obesity symbolized confidence—that without trying, he could naturally handle his own. The prison released Armando two days before.

"I was supposed to get out after four years, but some of the officials detected THC in my body and forced me to stay another seven months," he said. "I had my own flat-screen TV in my cell but didn't have anywhere to put it, so I smashed it when I left."

"You broke it on purpose?" I asked. *Why would someone break a TV on purpose?*

"Yeah. I didn't want any of those other fuckers to use it." His nostrils flared. "Man, it's so different going from the pen to a shelter. I have so many crazy thoughts right now." I tilted my head, urging him to continue. "I hate it here, man. So many people try to get up in my business and try an' tell me what I did wrong. We all messed up somewhere because we're here. Maybe you should look more at yourself instead of others. Focus on you and you changin'. I don't like the people. I want to take a MAC-10 or something and take everyone out."

"What?" I murmured to myself under my breath. I didn't know how to react. I had never found myself in a situation where someone admitted to me that they wanted to take a gun and shoot everyone. It overwhelmed me, and I froze.

He heard me and snickered. "I'm kidding." I didn't know whether to believe him or not. "When I was in the pen, I tried to find God. Others knew, so when I swore or something, they'd call me out on it. It's like, come on, we're all humans and make mistakes." He posed like a thinking statue, looking toward the ceiling briefly.

"Why is it that we only change our lives when something dramatic or tragic happens?" He turned back to me. "Being out feels good, though. Today, I ate a gyro and an Italian beef sandwich. Man, it tasted so good. It's those small things, you know?"

"I can imagine." I wondered what my first food craving would be out of prison. I loved gyros. Not having the opportunity to eat one in four years would probably make me scarf one down within first sight. I understood what he meant by "small things" more and more.

Armando continued, "You know, guys have no problem hittin' up girls, but then they never want to take care of the kids. I'm gonna take care of my kids and woman." He pressed his thumb to his chest. "I got a son and two daughters."

I smiled and pointed to gray marks I saw. "What're those on your hands?"

"I've been mixing concrete the last two days. I'm gonna work hard and provide for my family. I know I messed up, but I want to make it better now," he said. "I run into guys who try to show off their money to me. They flash me their Western Union slips like I'm supposed to care." He shook his head with a twisted face. "They should be trying to impress their family, their woman, or their kids." He paused and then reflected aloud to me again, "And why is it when you're on the streets, people drive by and automatically think you're a gangbanger or dangerous?"

"People just want a slice of information to justify their thoughts. It's easier to stereotype," I said.

He sighed. "Yeah, you're right."

We walked back to the main room together. The mats lay in place, and Andre was about to call names.

I made an effort to think more about what Armando experienced. He went straight from prison to a homeless shelter. He already had problems with people, which surprised me. Maybe the people in the shelter were similar to prison, or maybe Armando just interpreted it that way. He had a lot of pent-up frustration and anger, but he didn't know where to direct it. His transition from prison to "freedom" seemed to give him time to reflect on life and what was important to him. He was curious—perhaps curious to find a new way to live life.

Journal Entry — September 15, 2011

Hearing conversations about gangbangers and drugs has become a regular thing. Verbal arguments aren't out of the ordinary, but it's not a routine thing, either. I overhear which shelters the dope boys stay and which areas the gangbangers are at. I heard one guy say, "Weed is on Adams, blow is on Pulaski, and you can get anything between Hamlin and Cicero." I'll be honest—I'm taken aback. I'm not used to being around it. It makes me nervous and heightens my awareness. Although, I don't think I'll get caught in between anything. I just mind my business. If I think someone's approachable or cool, I'll say something or joke with them. Active listening is important.

CHAPTER EIGHT

THE VETERANS

"Hey, what's the deal with that Ozzy guy?" A man named Maurice scooted over by Max and me in the Inspired Horizons cafeteria and shielded his mouth from people standing in the breakfast line. "I saw him making out with some woman yesterday."

Max and I grimaced. "Don't put that image in our heads," Max whined. We could see Ozzy sitting alone three tables away. All around were men, women, and children with trays of food in front of them. The women and children always seemed in a hurry, like they had somewhere to be.

It wasn't the first time people asked about Ozzy. People asked about Rawls a lot too. Guys who stayed at the Gym possessed a natural curiosity about Rawls and what happened there. Their excited wonder humored me. They waved farewell the night before and then huddled around us the next day to hear the tales.

"That's his wife," Max replied to Maurice. "They're both part of the Horizons program but have to stay at separate shelters. Maybe that's why they're so attached when they're here."

"I saw him near the bathroom this morning with three bottles of pills. Whatever he's taking, his wife must be too," Maurice said.

Max shrugged. "Yeah, I don't know if they're taking them as they're prescribed or what. I used to work in the emergency room. Most people in other countries take them as they're prescribed, but in America, people take them for fun. Responsible people take them like they're supposed to, but pharmaceutical companies pay doctors to give them to their patients. Sometimes, I tore up patients' prescriptions because I knew they didn't need them—and that's how I lost my license." He chuckled. "One time, my ex had a stomachache and went to the doctor and came back with Nexium. I told her, 'No way are you taking that!'" He scolded with his finger. "It's ridiculous." He threw his arms in the air.

"That ain't right," Maurice said. "They're messing with people's lives, you know?" He shook his head.

"Another time, after my night shift, I went to cross the street to IHOP and a car hit me going forty miles an hour. I never believed people's shoes fell off, but sure enough, one of my high tops was gone." He laughed in a reminiscing fashion. "I didn't remember much in the hospital—just seeing a headlight and then waking up. I told the nurses not to give me any morphine—only eight hundred milligrams of ibuprofen. They were amazed I knew so much. They must not have seen my scrubs outfit I wore when the car hit me."

"I've seen so many people here with bottles of prescription drugs," I said to Max. "One night at Rawls, I saw a guy dump a bag onto the table and seven bottles spilled out. There's no way all those can work together, right?"

"No." He shook his head. "And when you're taking all of those, you try to cover up problems you have, but it can affect your body and mind. Say, your capability to navigate your way through your homeless situation."

I glanced toward Ozzy. He chewed on a peanut butter and jelly sandwich and washed it down with coffee from a Styrofoam cup. Someone tried to pass him and bumped his chair. He reacted slowly and clumsily. *Was it from the pills?* Luckily for him, two people worked at changing his situation: him and his wife. Two people working together to solve a problem usually was better than one.

We plopped our bags on the chairs next to us. I looked to the corner of the room. There was no noise. The rope was tied tighter to the wall. I exhaled.

Two men sat across the table from me.

"You must've been in the military," a man named Pete said to the tall black man with high cheekbones and braided hair.

"Army."

"Your posture gave you away." Pete smiled. The black man's bright smile lit up the room. "I don't have that anymore. My body's shit—SEALs."

The black man, Julius, nodded.

"Hey, everyone!" Keon waved his arms in the air. We turned our attention toward the shower line, forty feet away. "We don't have soap or towels tonight, so showers aren't mandatory."

"Aw, man." Julius shook his head. "I wanted to take one tonight. I've been sleeping in parks for a while." Pete and I watched Julius scratch his face. "I got sensitive skin. I don't have any soap or towels, so I was hoping they'd have it here."

"You need soap?" I asked.

"Yeah."

I grabbed my backpack, unzipped a compartment, and dug through the clothes. "Aha!" I pulled out a boxed bar of soap. "I bought this earlier today. Use it." I handed it to Julius. "If you need it, keep it."

He gave me a sincere, focused stare, extending his arm to shake my hand. "That's great of you, man. Thank you. I just got *such* sensitive skin. I've been scratching my face and my whole body these last couple days. I really appreciate it."

Some guys had money to buy simple things like soap, shampoo, and snacks, but others didn't. People looked after each other, especially if they knew the person needed something. I was glad to do what I could.

"Listen up, y'all!" Andre announced, dragging himself to the middle of the room. He rotated 180 degrees, making eye contact with everyone. "We don't have any bedsheets tonight."

Grunts and sighs filled the room.

"I know, I know. But y'all have 'em tomorrow night," Andre promised.

His assurance didn't quell the angst. The showers were one thing, but lying on a clean—at least we assumed—bedsheet was more important to guys, including myself. Few trusted the cleanliness of the mats. We witnessed volunteers drag them from a closet and the next morning, we hauled them back to the same closet. The probability someone washed them in between that time was undoubtedly low.

"Crazy." Pete shook his peppered black hair. He stayed on and off at Rawls in the past. "Still the same as before." He returned his focus to Julius. "Were you stationed anywhere?" he asked.

"Germany. For a number of years," Julius answered. "I feel like those guys are my brothers." Pete nodded. "You've been all over, I'm sure," Julius said.

"Yeah. You name it, I've probably been. Shook two presidents' hands too: Jimmy Carter and Ronald Reagan. They were both cool. Jimmy was so nice, though—and that was his problem."

Julius flashed a delightful smile. "That's neat."

Pete confessed, "What's *not* neat is carrying eight body bags in Iran. The only way you could tell the difference between the bodies was the color of their skin. They were just random cut-up and burned body parts." Julius and I lost expression in our faces. It sounded like something during the Iran Hostage Crisis.

Is he talking about Operation Eagle Claw? The Iran Hostage Crisis happened more than eight years before I was born. I didn't know much about it, except that a mission went wrong and people died. It was a big reason Jimmy Carter lost the presidency.

"Thank you," I said, not knowing how else to respond.

He slowly nodded his head, pursing his lips. Finally, he let out a long exhale.

Pete was a serviceman involved in one of the most infamous military operations in American history, and I met him not at a celebrated event that trumpeted his dedication to our country, but in a homeless shelter on the west side of Chicago. He matched the condition of the run-down shelter; his overaged body lumbered around, aching with each step from years of wear and demand, causing an unnatural waddle. Miraculously, hopeful smiles shown through his tough exterior and, along with whatever emotional baggage, he carried a contagious positive attitude. Rawls contained a similar spirit and heart, a pride from just being itself.

"Do you have a razor, Rick?" Armando asked. I stood in front of the sink brushing my teeth. "If so, can I use it?"

I smiled with a mouthful of toothpaste. "You think I actually have a razor?" I sloshed at him.

"Yeah, I guess you're right." He laughed. "You talk to your mom yet?"

I spit into the sink. Toothpaste stuck to my beard. I reached for a paper towel, tore off a piece, and wiped my mouth. "No. Not yet."

"All right. Just keep at it." He walked out of the bathroom.

Armando remembered what I told him about my situation and seemed genuinely concerned. I remained standing in front of the sink, noises from the third stall briefly interrupting my thinking.

The dirty mat stared directly back, challenging me. I tilted my head in hope of a new perspective. *What's the best way to lie on it without a bedsheet?* There was no good way. My only hope was to reduce as much contact between my skin and the mat. I layered up with clothes and kept my shoes on.

The man next to me walked to Andre, who was twenty feet away in the center of the room.

"Do you know where the nearest hospital is?" the man asked a stone-faced Andre.

"Uh, I'm not really sure. I haven't been here too long," Andre replied. "What do you need?"

"I'm going to cut my wrists," the man said point-blank.

Andre's mouth hung open. His eyes widened in disbelief. "You're going to cut your wrists," Andre repeated. The man nodded. "Hold that thought for a minute. I'll be right back!" He turned to his office, abandoning his typical monotonous pace for a hurried jog.

Guys whispered to the person next to them. Though the lights remained off, shuffled movement prevented anyone from falling asleep. Even for Rawls, the moment was out of the ordinary.

Minutes later, an ambulance parked outside and two police officers escorted the man up the shelter staircase. Andre stood outside his office door with a spacey gaze and breathed a sigh of relief.

The man felt so desperate that he wanted to cut his wrists. It was another instance reminding me of the serious issues many of the men dealt with. I tried to imagine the burden he carried, but I couldn't do anything—only hope he received the help he needed. Homelessness wasn't their biggest problem; they battled internal demons every minute of the day. The man's bravery to speak up to

Andre demonstrated courage.

I was proud of Andre for handling the situation with professionalism. I felt secure when he managed the shelter, unlike the substitute manager who allowed chaos to thrive and lacked empathy for others. He focused on the power of his position, abusing his authority to deliver long-winded rants, and scolded individuals for trivial matters. Andre toed the line of casual friendliness, yet remained stern when necessary. He made people feel safe and welcomed. He was a true leader.

The mat no longer intimidated me. I plopped myself down and exhaled into the night.

Journal Entry — September 18, 2011

Being homeless makes everything difficult—from treating a mental issue to maintaining hygiene. I feel more stressed from the constant chatter of gang violence and drugs, eating bad food like the soggy spaghetti tonight at Rawls, not showering and having no bedsheets, and the vulnerability to illnesses from people coughing throughout the whole night. Above all else, surprisingly, the repetition of everything is taking the biggest toll. I feel like I've gradually been stripped of my freedom. I never thought I'd be able to imagine how prison felt, but now, it seems easier to understand. The order and structure tire me. Having to be at particular places at specific times is a drag. Each day moves slower and slower. Earlier, someone at Inspired Horizons asked me how long I'd been here. I told him about two weeks. He warned me not to stay any longer. "These places will make a sane man crazy." Well, I guess I'll find out. My mental burden is certainly increasing.

CHAPTER NINE

I BRING YOU UP?

Like usual, I turned the corner from Broadway to avoid the red line Wilson exit. Armando walked toward me, carrying a small black bag. "You want a beer, Rick?"

"Sure," I said.

I followed Armando around the corner I had just come from. We walked below the rusted L tracks to a boarded-up, abandoned building. Weeds grew through cracks in the concrete. Paint chips fell from the elevated track when the train screeched to a stop.

Armando removed a twenty-four-ounce Icehouse beer from the bag. "Here." He handed me the beer.

Crack. I opened the can with my dirtier-than-usual fingernails. He opened the second beer and left the plastic bag on the ground before a slight breeze blew it away.

We stood exposed, seen by anyone who drove or walked past, but it was such a deserted spot that the eye naturally glanced over us. We sipped our beers. Cheap beer never tasted so good. I hadn't had alcohol in over a month.

He revealed a salt-packet-sized bag from his pocket. "This weed is real good, man. I know where to get the best." I laughed out loud. *That's what every drug dealer says.* "You have to watch out for these guys in here because they'll try to trick you. They hustle you with their bad weed and jacked prices."

A cop car passed. Armando quickly hid his beer behind his stiff leg, while I continued, naïvely, holding mine blatantly visible.

"You gotta hide that when the police go by. Use your head." I bobbed my head up and down. Armando was hyperaware. He was on parole for seven months and couldn't afford any run-ins with authorities. "You don't come from a background like the other guys at the shelter, do you?" he asked.

I shrugged. "I guess not."

"It's not a bad thing. It's just interesting—probably a good thing," he said encouragingly. "Get outta here as soon as you can." He took another swig from his can. "Any word from your family?"

"Still nothing," I said, surprised by how invested he was.

"You know, if it doesn't work out with your mom, you can always go out and make your own life."

I smiled to one side, nodding my head.

We finished our beers. Armando threw his empty can on the ground. He raised his eyebrows.

"What?" I asked.

"Your beer." He pointed to the can in my hand.

I shrugged. "I don't know. I was going to throw it in the garbage."

He chuckled. "Throw it on the ground. Make it look old—like it's been here a while. Kick some dirt on it."

"Oh. Okay." I tossed it on the ground and stepped on it with my discolored white shoes.

He sighed. "Man, you and I come from *very* different backgrounds."

On my walk back to the dayroom, I stopped in the garage. "You're Luis, right?" I asked a black man with a buzz cut. He was by himself. Six others were scattered in other places. He stood up from an upside-down bucket.

"Yeah!" He smiled, revealing a mouth of crooked teeth. Others told me he took antipsychotic drugs, but it didn't worry me. He seemed like a fun guy. I usually saw him in the dayroom, bouncing from table to table to talk with people.

Delighted that I knew his name, he offered me a cigarette but paused. "Ah, you don't look like you smoke." Others had said it before too. Not wanting to come across as straightedge, I grabbed it.

"I'll take one," I said. He smiled again. I borrowed his lighter, which had tigers on it. "I haven't seen a lighter like this. Everyone's are plain colors."

"Oh yeah! Anything with a cat on it. I love cats." He bent down and pointed to his black shoes. "A puma is a cat too."

I twisted my body to display my shoes to him. "Yours are better than mine." He chuckled. My shoes were from high school. I found them in the attic. They were a pair of white generic Reeboks. Over the past month and a half, they became a stained yellow. "Oh well."

I looked up back at Luis and lit the cigarette with a click.

"They're cheap ones," he confessed. "A pack costs a dollar twenty-five. I get 'em at the store at the end of the alley."

"Thank you." I bowed. "You're a gentleman."

"You think I'm a gentleman?" His cheeks turned red.

"From what I've known of you so far, yes," I replied.

He shook his head. "You wouldn't have thought I was a gentleman before. I was a crackhead for fourteen years. I stopped after I was in jail for the fifteenth time."

"That fifteenth time is the real tipping point," I joked, puffing out a cloud of smoke.

Luis laughed. "If you knew me before, you would've wanted to hit me on the head with a hammer. I've been sober since July twenty-seventh, though. It's not long, but it's something."

"It is, man." I put my hand on his shoulder. "You should be proud."

He blushed again. I finished my cigarette, and Luis quickly handed me another. I appreciated it. Not everyone would do that. I stuck it behind my right ear to save for later, but more importantly, to signal to others I wasn't straightedge.

I climbed the steps in the garage, entering the dayroom.

Max sat behind the volunteer table. I hadn't seen him much since he began staying at the Gym.

"Oh, Max. Look at you. You're on the other side now, eh?" I joked. His face didn't change.

"Now you're smoking, Rick?" He pointed to the cigarette behind my ear. "First you started drinking coffee more than usual, now this?"

I leaned back, appearing to look casual. "Hey, I smoke on occasion," I said defensively. I didn't see a reason for him to address me like that.

Lenny approached us at the table. "Hey, Rick. How're ya?"

"I'm fine, thanks," I replied awkwardly. His authority jolted our interaction; I felt my body shifting to an erect posture. A couple days prior, the messy, disorganized kitchen served as an office space where Lenny and I had a conversation. As the case manager, his job was to know each individual and their situation in order to understand how to serve them best.

He worried about my age. He expressed that he didn't like seeing people under the age of twenty-five, preferring they stay in youth shelters because of the gang activity in the area. Additionally, he warned me about being white in an all-black neighborhood where Rawls was. I told him what everyone else already knew—that I was holding out until the holidays, believing it was when I'd be able to return to Wisconsin.

I asked him how long guys could stay, and he laughed in my face. He said he tried to put a limit on it when he first got there, but the higher-ups squashed it. By the end of our conversation, I felt disheartened for him. A man passionate about helping others found himself caught in the bureaucracy of it all. Instead, he served individuals on a more intimate basis, referring people to services and providing small things like laundry cards.

Reggie burst through the shelter doors. "Man, everybody in here's huddled up, whining about the weather, and it's only September! There's gonna be some cryin' in this hallway when it's below zero in a bit." I smirked, but the disgruntled faces around me wiped it off.

"Rick, you're quiet," Elias noted, standing near me.

"I'm just minding my own business—that's all."

Armando interjected, "He may be quiet, but when you get to know him, he talks a lot."

I shot a sup nod to Armando, then reached into my backpack for a piece of gum.

Farouk noticed. "Can I have one?" He held out his hand.

"Sure." I placed a spearmint-flavored stick in his marked-up hand. I didn't mind sharing with him if it meant concealing his ashy breath. "When you're making out with a girl, they'll be like, 'Ooohh, Farouk, your breath is so fresh!'"

He giggled and reached into his pocket. He pulled out a gold dollar coin and gave it to me. "Look, you're rich now."

I took the coin and studied it for a moment. "Where'd you get this?" I asked.

"I got it today—downtown," he said as he thrust his chest and lifted his heels.

"How much did you make?"

"Forty-six dollars. I'll use it for my phone bill." He rummaged through his pocket again and removed another gold dollar coin. "I accidentally spent a few."

"Accidentally spent them? What'd you mean?" I asked.

"I like keeping them as souvenirs."

"Souvenirs, Farouk?"

He held the coin close to his face, staring at its shininess. "Mhm. So shiny you can see yourself."

It felt good to have camaraderie with others. I moved beyond the stage of initial meeting. I wasn't at zero anymore, like the first day when I sat in the dayroom waiting for the van. I wasn't intimidated anymore. Friends distracted me from homelessness. It was easier to experience shelter life with people I knew by my side.

I routinely made my way to the shower line, but Reggie disoriented me. He had an eagerness about him, like he'd been waiting for this moment.

"I got the money for you, Rick!" I forgot that a few days earlier, Reggie pulled me aside and asked to borrow a CTA pass. "I'm sorry it took me so long to pay you back."

"Ah, don't worry about it, man. I don't want your money." Reggie jerked his head back. "You're a good guy, Reggie. You're funny. Whenever you're around, you make me laugh."

He thought for a moment. "I bring you up?" he asked.

"Yeah. A lot of times, you help me get through the day. I love when you're around." I moved closer to the shower line. Reggie followed behind.

"So I bring you up?" he asked rhetorically with sparkling eyes.

"That means a lot. I appreciate that."

I smiled and gave a quick nod. "It's no problem. It's true. When I see you off in the distance, snapping your fingers, I think, 'Oh yeah, here comes Reggie. My day is all good from here.'"

"Ha, ha!" Reggie shouted, dancing in a circle. He clapped his hands loudly. "Man, that feels so good. You know, sometimes I'm just so depressed." He quickly hung his head and gripped my shoulder. "The other day when I was at the VA, I asked if anyone had a pistol to shoot myself."

"What!" I gasped. I experienced a moment of breathlessness. I shook my head in disbelief, but Reggie only laughed.

"Relax, Rick. I just said it so they would take me in quicker," he elaborated. I didn't believe him. Reggie appeared detached from the world from time to time. I worried about him and wondered if he ever received help from anybody at the VA. I paused for a few moments to collect myself.

"I didn't know you were a veteran," I said.

"Yeah, the navy in the early eighties. I was on . . ." Reggie began listing the names of all the ships he served on. To me, they sounded like random words and numbers, but he made deliberate, stiff gestures with his hands, unwilling to be anything but specific, and locked eyes with me so intensely that I practically fell backward.

"What was that like?" I asked. He returned to his infamous, animated storytelling.

"One time I was in the bathroom of the ship, and this redneck from Arkansas started talkin' trash to me." Reggie altered his voice to create an over-the-top trashy southern accent. "I'mma break out a barrel of whoop-ass and kick your ass, Reggie!" He stood in a boxing stance, exaggerating the lameness of the man.

"I walked toward him and said, 'Oh, no you're not!'" Reggie punched the air twice. "*Pop! Pop!*"

Reggie looked down at the concrete tiles. "He tried getting up, but I stood over the top of him—like this." He got into position, showing me exactly what his stance was like back then. "I said, 'If you get up, I'm just going to knock you back down.'"

He changed his voice again to a wimpy cry. "'Ah, ah! Reggie punched me. I told him I was going to whoop his ass, and he punched me first,' that redneck bitched."

My dimples ached from laughing. Reggie fervently acted out the scene, flailing his arms with relentless footwork. Others around us observed with grinning faces.

"That guy just got a slap on the wrist." Reggie pounded on a metal chair. "While I was only paid half for two months. On top of that, I spent thirty days in the brig—the jail inside the ship. Ain't that some bullshit."

I patted him on the back, shaking my head with a smile. I never met a person more entertaining than Reggie.

"We got too many guys here tonight," bellowed Andre in front of everyone sitting in chairs, leaned against the kitchen wall. "If you want to leave, you can. I won't hold it against you." Once signed in, no one could leave until after two in the morning. It wouldn't be fair if someone only ate and left, using a space someone else could use. If someone broke the rules, Andre slapped them with a ban. The length depended on the severity of each situation.

No one volunteered, so Andre sweetened the deal. "If any of you want to leave, I have a cigarette waiting for you at the door." Suddenly, heads shot up. "And I'll throw in five bucks—actually two."

"I'll leave for five," someone said aloud.

Andre made his way to my area. He looked at Pete, sitting next to me.

"Sure you don't want to go back to the north side?" Andre asked Pete.

"Nah, I'm good." Pete laughed. Andre turned his focus to me.

"Slick Rick! How you doin'? Rick's a smooth guy, y'all," Andre expressed to the room. I felt my face turn red from the attention. Andre continued, "If I had sixty guys like Rick, this place would be the best—it'd be so easy for me."

I shrugged. "I'm just doin' my thing, you know."

"You sure you don't want to go back by Horizons, Rick?"

"Nah. I'm good too."

Moments later, two men volunteered to leave for two dollars and a cigarette each. Volunteers finished mopping the floor and brought out the mats.

Andre held the sign-in clipboard to his face, gazing at it casually. "Listen up, y'all," he shouted to us. "I'm gonna do somethin' unprecedented," he explained with wide arms.

"What's that mean?" a guy hollered back to him.

"Something new that's never been attempted before," Andre

answered. "I'm in such a good mood, I'm gonna let y'all pick your beds."

A sleeping energy awoke. Applause ensued. Guys yelled. The room grew so loud that it shook the ceiling fans back and forth. Andre smiled with surprised delight; he stumbled upon an ingenious motivational tool.

"That's what I'm talking about!" someone yelled near me.

Like anything else, guys had their own preferences of beds. Some liked the security from physical objects like columns or walls; some liked the idea of sleeping next to friends; and some liked the larger, thicker mats compared to the common thin ones. Above anything else, it was freedom that Andre allowed. The idea was more powerful than a mat itself.

Andre still read in order of the sign-in sheet but created on-the-fly nicknames. "D-K. Marlboro Man. President McKinley. Jumpin' Jackson. Ozzy. Delicious Dave, Cupid Quigley, the Three Amigos, Jackie Chan."

"He's actually Mongolian—not Chinese." The man sitting near me rolled his eyes. It was the first instance of political correctness in the shelter. It wasn't a high priority. After spending four years in a collegiate environment, I found it refreshing. To be honest, the guys at the shelter reminded me of the guys I grew up with in Wisconsin. They razzed and teased each other. It was part of the culture. To fit in, you needed thick skin and the ability to take jabs. No one got bent out of shape.

These guys wanted to just live their lives, unbothered by authorities and government. They didn't follow politics because it was the same thing every time—and the same type of guy standing in front, telling them what's wrong and how to fix it. Few in Wisconsin examined the nitty-gritty details of policies affecting them; they voted Republican because that was the culture. It was simply what you did. The guys at the shelter were the same. None of them read the fine print of policies affecting them, either; they voted Democrat because that was the culture. The two groups of guys seemed starkly similar in attitude and personality. It was only their backgrounds and environments that differed.

Journal Entry — September 22, 2011

I hope I'm more positive tomorrow. I'm just sick and tired of everything. This being homeless thing sucks. I wasn't feelin' it at all this morning. I want to be somewhere away from people, where I can relax by myself, with no distractions or worries of anything going on around me. Something as simple as a living-room chair or an actual bed would be heaven. In the last month and a half, I haven't had a private moment. I'm always in public or with other people, incapable to reflect in solitude. My inability to recharge causes the days to seem continuous and never-ending. I'm miserable right now. I wonder if other guys feel this way too. I sense they do.

I'm voluntarily homeless, seeking an understanding of what it feels like to be homeless. Many others are actively looking for jobs and housing. If I find it immensely challenging to recharge, reflect, and just think, then I wonder what it's like for them. Most don't stay every night at Rawls. They have friends or family to occasionally stay with, breaking up the week. They exert effort into the next step in their lives. Does that help them to stay more positive and focused instead of just waiting around like me? I don't know.

CHAPTER TEN

PRISON

We stood near a column by the kitchen wall. A few guys remained seated at the tables, finishing their dinner. Soon, the volunteers would sweep and mop the floor, and the nightly ritual would continue.

"Elias, how'd those workshops and stuff go?" I asked as he stood next to me.

"Oh, good! People helped me with my résumé, and I practiced interviews," he informed me. He touched my arm. "Your online image is a big thing these days too. There's a website called LinkedIn where you can put in your résumé and connect with others. You should look into it too. I'd bet it'd help you."

"I suppose," I said.

"I didn't get as much done as I wanted today, though," he admitted.

"Why's that?" I asked.

"I had to do laundry."

I nodded my head. "Yeah, I usually go to this Laundromat off the

Morse stop, up in Rogers Park."

"Oh, how come you go there?" he asked. "You know Lenny will give you tokens for the one by us, right?"

The men had finished their meals, and volunteers slid the folded-up tables underneath the stage. I momentarily watched one volunteer carelessly sweep the floor, then I turned back to Elias.

"Yeah, I know," I said. "I don't know. I've just gone to this one for a while. I like the people working there, I guess." I shrugged. I felt a sharp poke on my stomach.

"What's up, white boy?" Armando whispered, holding a switchblade to my skin.

"Ah!" I jumped back, clutching my stomach to ensure it was still intact. "The fuck, man? Don't do that shit!" My face pinched together. I became hot and energized, like I got a kick of adrenaline. It must've been my survival instincts.

Armando laughed, slapping his knee before putting away the switchblade. "I'm kidding."

I didn't care if he was "joking." It wasn't cool and, sometimes, pranks went wrong. *Did he do this to others or just me?* Before living homeless, I wondered if I'd get into situations like this. *And how'd he even sneak that inside? Rawls bans knives. Well, duh, volunteers skim bags without a care. Security is a joke.*

Elias glared at Armando side-eyed, uncharmed by his shenanigans too.

My gut told me Armando was testing me to see how I'd react. His calm casualness after the fact communicated that it was his own twisted experiment. Would I just lie down and take it, or would I become aggressive and hostile toward him? I tried to toe the line with a stern warning not to do it again.

"Just don't go to prison, Rick"—Armando waved his hand—"you're not a bad-looking guy. You probably won't ever go there, though. It's not as bad as it used to be. There's more protection than in the older days."

"Yeah?" I said, still glaring at him with a disenchanted look. A volunteer asked us to step back so he could sweep the area. We moved closer to the wall, where others sat on chairs.

Armando continued, "I remember the new guy in the cell next to me. On his first night, I heard him howl like it was a full moon. The next morning, he hobbled into the cafeteria. I asked him why he let his cellie rape him. He said he'd get extra food and soap and things." Elias openly stared at Armando. His hand palmed one side of his face. I swallowed with difficulty.

Armando's eyes looked different than usual. They weren't suspicious, and his matched smirk never appeared. Instead, they bulged from his face and his eyebrows drew together, almost as if he relived a moment in prison. He typically walked around Inspired Horizons and Rawls with a forced swagger, a front to fool guys he was hard. But during the conversation with Elias and me, he dropped the act and spoke truthfully. He appeared vulnerable, and I believed him.

"Being neutral can be tough. You don't have protection. Some gangs will be nice to you, and you're relieved. But it only takes one look from one gang member to another to jump you. That's why it was nice being affiliated." He held out both of his fists, revealing lines and dots tattooed below each knuckle.

Elias and I leaned forward and focused on the back on his hands. I didn't know what it meant. Were the lines and dots standard for his gang? Or did he have to earn every mark? I saw the scene he described over and over in the movies. *So I guess it is true.* I wondered what I'd do in prison. Staying neutral would assume a clean lifestyle, but joining a gang seemed crucial to survival.

Armando added, "Sometimes, there'll be one big guy who looks and acts like Superman when guys are fuckin' with someone—all righteous and everything. The guy will be like, 'Hey! This is a human being. Leave him alone!' The person will be so thankful he saved him. Then the big guy will pull him aside and say, 'You can either keep letting these guys mess with you or you can stick with me. Your decision.' So that guy becomes his bitch."

"Oh my goodness," eked Elias. He rubbed the back of his neck, clearly feeling uncomfortable. He looked pale and wobbled back and forth where he stood. Armando's stories made me feel uneasy too. The elevated heat was from anger before, but now, it was from anxiousness. A panicky tingle ran up my spine.

"It's like fishing," Armando said. "If you're not tough right away and stand up for yourself, they'll get a bite." His philosophy explained his persona around others. He adapted the defense mechanism in prison and continued it in the shelter. He created a tough-first impression to reinforce others to leave him alone. He was fishing earlier when he poked me with the switchblade.

I carefully floated to Curtis, leaning against the stage. Volunteers hauled mats and placed them a foot from each other. "Fantastic Voyage" played through the stereo, which juxtaposed Curtis's focused demeanor. I'd seen him over the past week, always alone, with his head buried in a stack of books. At the moment, four surrounded him, but I was sure his three bags, spread out on the stage, contained more. The notebook and pen in his hand made it look like he took inventory of his belongings.

"How many books have you read?" I asked.

He thought for a moment. "Probably over four hundred."

"Whoa!" My mouth gaped open. It seemed high, even though I hadn't the slightest idea how many I'd read over the years.

"Well, I was in prison," he explained as a humble excuse for the high achievement. "I was supposed to be in there for eighteen years but got out in six and three months. I got out early 'cause I earned two degrees: one in marketing and the other in criminal justice. I'd be stupid not to. You can get one from any number of schools. I also revisited my trial and found something to lessen my penalty."

"Do a lot of people read in there?" I asked.

"Many do. I would read about three books a week. There's nothing else to do."

Thinking back to my conversation with Armando, I brashly asked, "If you just mind your own business in prison, will people still mess with you?"

He responded in a direct but weary voice, "So many people are real defensive. They know nothing else but that. You could be by yourself and some guy will get in your face because, apparently, you 'looked' at him a certain way." Curtis rolled his eyes. "You have to put your foot down when you first get there so people don't take advantage of you. Otherwise, time will pass even slower." He clearly echoed Armando's philosophy.

I leaned even closer to Curtis and rested my hand on the stage. Small red paint chips clung to my palm. My hearing was poor, so I wanted to make sure I understood everything he said. He was a wise, no-nonsense guy. I didn't want to look foolish by asking him to repeat himself.

"There's this 'jail' inside prison referred to as 'the hole.' You aren't able to watch TV, hang out, go outside, or whatever else. You're locked in a real small cell for twenty-three hours of the day. No one wants to go there—that's the worst possible thing." He swiftly crossed his hands in front of his body. "Whatever you do, don't go around saying you only have five or whatever days left. While you're happy, there are people who've already been in jail for twenty-plus years and still have *life* to go. Just because you're prancin' around, excited to get out, they'll start a fight, sending both of you to the hole. Now you have to wait longer than those five days."

The subject of life sentences interested me. "I mean, if I got life in prison, I'd probably kill myself," I confessed to him. The thought of being caged for the entirety of my breathing life depressed me. Curtis, however, didn't flinch at all. He patiently nodded his head. It clearly wasn't the first time he'd heard that.

"I can see where you're coming from. That makes sense. But guys travel from one joint to another. They see so-and-so here and that person there." He pointed in the air. "They accept that this is their life and look for new ways to find purpose. Many read, some become more spiritual, and others talk to kids and teach them about decision-making. Physical boundaries don't mean your life is worthless."

Curtis connected the ideas in my head, allowing me to draw a parallel between prison and my experience in the homeless shelter. I found meaning in his explanation of life sentences. Around two weeks in the shelter, I noticed a shift within me. Calmness replaced my sharp vulnerability. My mind accepted that living homeless was my current life. Though voluntarily homeless, the thought of abandoning this new life never arose.

Journal Entry — September 26, 2011

I just don't know what to think sometimes. Armando is challenging to figure out. He's the only person I've interacted with who I'm not actually sure about. His behavior around me is hot and cold. Sometimes he's friendly toward me, asking if my family situation has improved. Other times, he's pulling a switchblade on me! I'm trying to avoid conflicts in the shelter, so I'm more passive than usual. I hate it. I'm not sure if Armando is just playing me or what. What's interesting, though, is that he mumbled, "We're not living—we're just existing." He's the fourth person I've heard say that phrase. He says he's working hard to get out of the shelter. I guess if I stop seeing him, I'll know things are improving. Armando's the least of my concerns, though.

I chose to live homeless because I thought it'd answer questions I was curious about. Instead, it feels like I have more questions. It pulls my emotions in different directions. For instance, I always imagined how much stress a single mother living in poverty endured. I felt bad for her. I wondered who these fathers were that left them alone—and I realized some of them are with me at Rawls.

Earlier, we waited for the volunteers to sweep and mop the floor. A man went on a loud rant. "We keep judging each other, when really, if we pulled our resources together, we could do some good. But no, mothers got it tough and have to raise kids by themselves. These kids have seven fathers. As fathers, we're not helping and our sons are paying for it."

"I know mine is!" another guy chimed in.

"So is mine!" yelled another.

"Instead of doing something, we're just trying to have fun. We're not trying to help out. We're going around trying to get our dicks sucked. A drink. A rock. A blow. Shit. I'm sixty and still having fun. Sure, I don't have a place and stay at Rawls, but after I get out, I can have fun."

It just really bothered me. And when I think about it, I might be friends with some of them. Well, actually, I don't know—most of the guys I hang around seem like good guys. They're flawed, of course, but so am I.

I can't stop thinking about this cycle. I don't have any answers. A child grows up with a stressed-out mother in a poor neighborhood; the public school sucks, so they're not getting a good education; without an education, their income opportunities are limited; they get busted selling drugs or for gang-related activities and end up in prison; and they get out and stay at Rawls. The cycle is way more complex than that—but that's what it looks like in my head, I guess. It feels hopeless without the intervention of an incredible individual or group.

Oh, and all of that is before society already stacked the deck against them. My views on the criminal justice system are rapidly changing. It's not that I had much of an opinion before, but talking with guys and listening to their stories makes me feel the system is heavy-handed with minorities. It's jacked up. Bullshit petty offenses stack up because police patrol more in minority neighborhoods, which eventually prevents them from getting jobs, leaving them homeless at Rawls.

CHAPTER ELEVEN

CLYDE

Pete and I waited next to each other in the shower line. He taught me how to play Sudoku. Each day, the *Chicago Red Eye* had a new puzzle. The difficulty progressed throughout the week and, after Monday and Tuesday, I needed Pete's constant help. He patiently guided me through the solutions. He told me I reminded him of his son. I was fond of him. The puzzles gave us something else to bond over, besides being homeless.

"What'd you get for the middle box in the lower-right square?" I asked Pete, leaning over his shoulder.

"Should be a seven," he said.

"Damn it. You sure it's not a five?"

He laughed. "I don't think so."

"Ugh."

"What're you working on?" Juan joined me in the shower line.

"Sudoku puzzle." I looked up. "I do it to pass the time." I pointed to Pete. "He does it because he's old and thinks it keeps his mind sharp."

Pete and Juan laughed. "Hey, I'm old too!" Juan said.

"Yeah, well, let's see how far you get without my help." Pete turned his body away from me, shielding the puzzle.

"Aw, come on. I was just saying a fact," I whined.

Pete smiled. "You like razzin' us, don't you?"

"It's my favorite thing to do to kill time," I said. "And when I do my puzzle with you, I kill two birds with one stone."

Juan dug into his dark-red backpack and pulled out a small brown paper bag. "You guys want a sandwich?" Juan extended his arm to us. "A van pulled up before you guys came. I think it was a church or something." Pete grabbed one. I waved a no-thank-you. I wasn't particularly hungry at the moment and didn't want to take one if it meant someone else couldn't eat it.

"Wow. That's pretty nice of them." I enjoyed discovering random acts of kindness. It made me more optimistic about people and the world.

"Yeah, a priest and a nun handed out these sandwiches and chips. They said they'd be back every week. I hope they are. The nun was cute."

I laughed. "Juan! Are you serious? A nun?"

Juan's face and ears turned red. His chest caved inward as he dipped his chin. "She was, though."

"You really are desperate, aren't you?" I asked.

"Yeah." Juan bashfully turned away.

"I need two! I need two!" Keon's voice carried in the background. Pete and I marched toward the showers, smiling back at Juan.

"Well, it looks like my gamble didn't pay off." Elias laughed, smiling so large his eyes grew narrow. I joined him at the table near the entrance.

Elias pointed to his plate. "Rice and beans again."

"Or as Juan calls them, dirt beans," I noted.

Elias and I had a running joke with each other. We often sat together at dinner in the Inspired Horizons cafeteria. More times than not, the food was bad. Each week was a rotation of freezer-burned chicken, some version of soggy tasteless noodles, rice and beans, half-frozen, half-warm ham circles, and fried veal—known more as "mystery meat" to guys in the shelter. Sometimes, we couldn't tolerate it, and we'd say to the other, "I'm betting on Rawls," on our way to the trash can. Rawls served slightly more tolerable food.

"Oh, come over here, Clyde." Elias waved joyfully to a tall black man.

He slowly walked toward us with an unyielding face. The closer he came, the clearer his chiseled features stood out. Veins popped from his toned body. A yellow bandana covered his shaved head. His large fierce eyes rested above his high cheekbones that, unlike Julius, made him appear frightening rather than charming. Smiling wasn't in his facial repertoire, only variations of frowns and deathly stares. All in all, he was the most intimidating man I ever saw. The contrast between him and Elias was enormous, though Elias had a friendly way about him that invited strangers with welcome arms.

Elias introduced us. "Clyde, this is Rick. Starting tomorrow, I won't be at Rawls anymore so now you'll know someone else here. I got into the housing above Horizons."

Clyde recently left prison after twenty-three years, almost half his life as a then forty-nine-year-old. His eyes were dull and blank. It looked like his soul was trapped inside his body. His muscles appeared unnaturally stiff, overexerting energy to hold his body up from defeat. His shoulders stuck out to me. They were wide but rigid, longing to slouch, but he couldn't control his body to look anything but tough. He expressed dissatisfaction with his family.

Clyde admitted, "It sucked when no one would come visit me in prison. I would write nine-page letters to them, and then all I got back was a card with one sentence. It is what it is, but at least I'm trying to be all right with them. Once I got out, I learned my brother's about to serve an eight-year sentence." He shook his head. "I talked to him most before and now, really, it's mainly my sister. She's trying to get to know the new me. I ate at her house earlier today, and I'm stuffed right now." He set his hand on his flat abdomen. Elias nodded with an understanding, closed-lip smile.

"Where're you from?" Clyde asked me with a heavy voice.

"Wisconsin. About twenty-five minutes south of Milwaukee."

"What's it like there?" he asked.

"Well, I don't know too much about the city. I'm from more of the rural parts, with open fields and everything. Milwaukee's probably like Chicago but a scaled-down version."

Clyde crossed his arms and rubbed his chin. "I'm thinking about moving somewhere and starting over. Milwaukee is one of the places I've thought about. I at least wanna go to an urban setting. I'd know how to adapt better with that. I've lived in Chicago my whole life and, if I stay, the only thing here for me is trouble. I'm trying to get away from all that." He sighed deeply. "At the same time, it'd be intimidating and difficult to just randomly move somewhere where you don't know anyone at all."

"Yeah, I can see that would be tough," I told him, even though his confession confused me. The most intimidating man I ever met was *afraid*. He feared change, even though he knew it'd help him.

"I don't want to be around a straight-based person who says shit when I do drugs—judging me and shit. But when I'm around people who do drugs, they can get crazy and start shit. That's when I get in trouble. I want to avoid all that drama and everything."

Apparently, Elias introduced him to someone earlier before me. Clyde didn't like that. "I understand that's the type of person you are, friendly and willing to go out of your way to help someone, but next thing you know, they'll want to be by me all the time and shit." He shifted in his chair. His tongue poked his cheek and he inhaled. "My idea of a good time is being in a hotel room for a night and watching TV. I'd get a forty-ounce to help me relax, and then I'd buy a phone card and call one of those singles hotlines until I find a girl who wants to freak."

Laughter spilled from my mouth. "People actually *call* those?"

He shot me a rigid glance. "Hell yeah."

I smiled back. Clyde fascinated me. A solid-hearted man trying to survive the infinite obstacles life threw at him.

CHAPTER TWELVE

WORRIED ABOUT REGGIE

An hour remained before roll call, yet someone (or their belongings) occupied each chair in the dayroom. I didn't want to snake my way through the crowd to get to the open hallway, so I leaned against the dull-colored wall, next to the garage door where I could see the TV.

A bootlegged DVD of *Abduction* played on the screen. Grown men gripped their seats in suspense, cheering the *Twilight* star, Taylor Lautner, as he chased through the streets of Pittsburgh.

I heard a mumbling voice near me. Reggie stopped in front of me. "And I said, 'I'm gonna have to pull some gangsta tricks.' You know what I mean, Rick?"

I pulled my eyes away from the thrilling scene. "What?"

Reggie never made eye contact with me or anyone. He stared beyond me, through me, with a spacey focus. He continued on his nonsensical rant. Since it looked like he was only talking to himself, I ignored him.

"Rick," he breathed, bringing me back into a conversation I wasn't involved in.

I witnessed this version of him before, but not as extreme. He frightened me—not for my safety, but for his. His hazy, out-of-body state grew darker and darker.

"My granddaddy worked on the chain gang and it made him cold, coldhearted!" Reggie stomped to keep my attention. "Our granddaddy wasn't blood—just someone our grandmamma remarried. And that man used to beat me and my brothers if we ever did anything wrong," he said. "We had two pistols in a closet hidden in a shoebox. My youngest brother, Jackson, was thirteen and threatened to shoot him. 'I don't care if I go to *hell*! I don't want to be beaten again!' he said. I had to calm him down."

"Jeez," I whispered. I wondered if Reggie got the scar on his cheek from his grandfather.

"I used to put a sheet of paper on the shoebox and lean a pencil against it to know if anyone fiddled with it. One time, I noticed a change, so I hid it again. I figured Jackson wanted the guns, so I had to stop him from getting to them. After a beating one time, my mother cried and pleaded to my granddaddy not to do it again. He called her a bitch and a hoe, and she got so upset that she took his oak wood cane and whacked him over his head."

I stood frozen with my jaw on the floor. *This is probably just one of the many painful memories he has*, I thought. I looked around, searching for an excuse to leave Reggie—to leave their awful conversation about things I could never imagine. I spotted Luis.

"Luis!" I called out as he walked past us. I jogged over to meet him, fleeing from Reggie. "Do you have a square?"

He grinned wider than his face. "Yeah." He had given me one

every day since I had met him. "You should stay at the Gym, Rick."

"There you go again, Luis. You're always trying to persuade me to stay there." I bounced closer to him and touched his arm. "You're a politician, you know."

"Me? A politician?" He laughed so hard that he couldn't keep his eyes open or his tongue from hanging out of his mouth. "You're the real politician!" he accused me with his pointed finger.

"What?" I shouted in a comic disbelief.

"I see you every morning with three bowls of cereal. Politicians always charm their way through a situation and come out with more than everyone else."

I bobbed my head up and down with a shit-eating grin. "You got me there," I admitted.

"I just think it'd be cool if you were at the Gym too. We'd have fun." He spoke sincerely. "But in a couple more weeks, I probably won't be there. I've been working with my caseworker. She's really nice. And I'll be getting a place and some money."

"Oh, that's awesome, man."

"Yeah, I've been working with the hospital psych department. They said I'm welcome back anytime. They love me because they think I'm crazy." He nudged me, bursting into laughter. I couldn't help but join him.

"We're the youngest ones here," Jarris said.

"And you're four under me," I said. From the shower line, we scanned the room full of grown men.

Jarris and I had been acquainted for a couple weeks. We saw each other at Inspired Horizons and sometimes rode the van together. He'd been an orphan since he was twelve years old. But he was now eighteen, medium height, and had corn-rowed black hair. His shiny earring studs reminded me I'd never be as cool as him.

"What brought you to a place like this?" I asked.

"My older brother left town for Tennessee. His girl didn't want me staying with them, so I'm homeless."

"That's shitty of them."

He shrugged. "Eh, it is what it is. I'll be fine. In four years, I want to be out of Chicago, anyway. But first, I'm going to finish school."

"How much do you have left?"

"Only a year."

"Gotcha." I tried to encourage him. "Yeah, the difference between us and everyone is that we still have a lot of life ahead of us."

"And I ain't gonna be livin' paycheck to paycheck like these guys." He motioned with the free hand of his crossed arms. "Some of these guys try to bring me under their wing, saying they can protect me and help me if I join their gang. I ain't about that. And then you have some guys, like this guy the other day . . ." Jarris switched to a mocking voice. "'I know this guy who has a shipping company. He can put you on payroll and give you four thousand dollars. When you file taxes, you'll get back money from the government. The guy knows accounting and everything.'" Jarris rolled his eyes. "Get outta here with that shit. Go try and scam some other fool."

Jarris and I got along well. I admired him. His overwhelming positive qualities jumped at me. His independence, ambition, and intelligence were obvious. He figured out more about life than I had at his age. I didn't worry about him at all.

"Rick," Vinny called. I had just brushed my teeth and began walking back to my chair against the wall. "You wanna watch the Bears game on Sunday at a bar?"

I curled my lips in disinterest. It seemed like a ploy to get me to hang out with him outside the shelter. The only other time I saw him was at the Saturday breakfasts. The nearby church put on a spectacular meal. Cereal, grits, hash browns, toast, sausage, and orange juice. The volunteers made us feel especially welcomed, like we were all a community. Vinny and his dad always joined Juan, Elias, Pete, and me. But I didn't know if I wanted to do something else with him. I didn't even care about the Bears, and I definitely didn't want to spend money.

We walked slowly toward everyone else, waiting for the volunteers to prepare the floor. "I can't really afford it right now, man." I lowered my head.

"That's fine. I'll pay for you."

My ears perked up. "Is that so?"

"Yeah. Come on." He waved. "It'll be fun. We'll get out of this environment for a bit and eat a good meal for once."

He was right. It would've been nice to get away from everything. And my stomach had forgotten that not all food was mass-prepared.

We arrived at my chair. My backpack was on top. I opened the front pouch, removed my Ziploc toiletries bag, and put my toothbrush back.

"Juan's coming too," he said. My head shot up to meet Vinny's eyes. *Sold.* Juan would alleviate the awkwardness.

"All right. I'll go."

"Cool. We'll meet at the bar, C 162. It's right across Wrigley Field. Do you have a phone? You can call if something comes up."

"No. I don't have a phone," I said.

"What?" he balked at me, his mouth hanging open.

"I don't have a phone," I repeated.

"How do you *not* have a phone?" This fact blew his mind. A twenty-two-year-old didn't have a cell phone—not even a cheap flip phone or one that looked like a brick.

I shrugged. "I figure it out," I said. "If I ever run into an emergency, everyone else around me already has one."

He shook his head, squinting his eyes. Asking more follow-up questions to me about it would've confused him more, so he turned and began walking away. "But I'll see you at the bar, right?" he asked over his shoulder.

"Yeah, I'll be there," I replied. His bull-legged walk turned into a skip. It made me smile.

Vinny wasn't the only one who asked for my phone number. They each mirrored Vinny's disbelieving response. Everyone had cell phones. The days leading up to when I became homeless, I was so adamant not to have a phone. Part of it was thinking a homeless individual wouldn't have a phone, and part of it was just that I wanted to do without it—to drop off the grid and observe what it was like. Each time someone asked me for my phone number, it reminded me of my naïve presumption. For many in the shelter, however, it was crucial to get in contact with potential housing providers or employers, or family and friends.

I admit, though, not owning a cell phone provided an interesting twist during conversations. Guys forgot what life was like before them. They asked me how I managed my life. I informed them I never showed up late as a result, and I always asked for specific times and places to meet. People-watching grew more interesting, and small things like a robin struggling to catch a worm on the sidewalk became noticeable to me.

Andre walked from his office to the center of the room. He put his hands around his mouth. "Listen up y—" His eyebrows lowered and a scowl appeared on his face. He stormed to the kitchen wall. "Jenkins! What're you doing here? I barred you for five days!"

"But I—"

"You were sleeping naked!" Andre yelled. The room roared with laughter. Guys turned to their neighbors with open-mouthed smiles. An overweight man near me fell off his chair laughing, bracing his fall with his wrist. "I'll let you stay the night, but after that, don't come back for a few days." The man nodded and stared at the ground. "On another note," Andre continued, "the reason why I came out here is because there were fifteen bars of soap left in the shower tonight. Y'all talk about how much you want them, but then y'all just leave 'em there!"

I felt a wave of guilt engulf me. I left one of the fifteen bars. It was the first time I used soap from Rawls. Mine was small. I wanted to conserve it until I bought a new one. *How was I supposed to know Andre would make a big deal about it?*

CHAPTER THIRTEEN

THE LIBRARY

"Juan!" I waited at the bottom of the Harold Washington L stop for a hobbling Juan. The weather was nicer than it had been the last few days. The sun warmed my face. We began our short, one-block journey to the library. "What's going on with your leg?" I pointed to his limped stride.

He lowered his head and grabbed his left calf. "It's an injury acting up from years ago," he explained. "I used to play baseball in high school. I was quick, you know, so I played centerfield. One time, I stepped into a pothole and broke my ankle."

I smiled. "A pothole did that to ya, huh?"

"That stupid thing has been laughing at me for forty years!" He shook his head, smirking. He flashed a package in front of my face. "You want these crackers? I was just at 7-Eleven," he said. "I got this sandwich too." He opened his plastic bag and revealed a ham-and-cheddar sandwich."

"Sure. Thanks. These kind of crackers are my favorite."

We reached the heavy library door, and I dumped the last remnants of my snack into my mouth and wiped my greasy hand on my jeans. I heaved the door open for Juan. "After you, sir."

"Oh," he chuckled, "thank you, young man."

The Harold Washington was the main library in the city. It was a brown monstrosity. It was built in the early 1990s and its ornamentation had turned green over the years. A kindergarten art class could have figured out that brown and green made a horrible color combination. The inside felt like a city itself. I found myself lost on several occasions. The tall shelves packed with dusty books created mazes that required their own map. Each genre had its own floor.

Juan and I made our way up two escalators to the third floor. The security guard gave us a sup nod, recognizing us from our separate, frequent visits. I remember feeling embarrassed when he first asked me to open my bag to check for stolen books. All he found were clothes and toiletries. He uttered an "oh" under his breath because he realized I was homeless. Since then, he barely checked; sometimes, he didn't even ask me to open it.

The third floor was the main floor, bustling with people. Four one-hundred-foot-long rows of computers dominated one area. Juan and I found a table tucked in a cove. I threw my backpack down on a chair by the wall. It made a loud thud.

"Oh, anxious, are we?" His large eyes lectured me. He neatly placed his backpack on the chair next to him.

"I just like having the wall or something behind me. I'm paranoid like that," I said.

The library interior and furniture looked unchanged since its opening. It was as close to a time capsule of the '90s interior design trends that I could imagine. Everything was twice as large as it needed to be and three times heavier than it needed to be. Two people could've sat on my uncomfortable chair. Lots of turquoise and pink. The blond wood's edges had become rounded over the years of use. The light-blue carpet was worn and its seams were frayed. Parts of some large square carpet tiles lifted over, revealing the glue job below it.

Juan pulled a large hardcover book from his backpack. John Lennon's face spread over the cover, wearing his iconic eyeglasses. It struck me how different it was from the usual science-fiction novels he read at Rawls.

"You like the Beatles, Rick?"

"Yeah, definitely. They're one of my favorites."

"What's your favorite album?" he asked.

"Hmm. Probably the White Album."

"Oh, yeah, that's a really good one. Mine's Sgt. Pepper's. I was eighteen when it came out. I listened to it all the time. It was so different than anything I heard before. That album revolutionized music, you know."

"I heard that it did. I don't really know what that means, though," I confessed.

Juan leaned forward with a focused posture. "Their tours became a circus. People protested, they had death threats, they couldn't even hear their music because girls screamed so loud!" he explained. "So they put all their effort into their next album. They experimented and recorded sounds that couldn't be performed live. It was the first concept album."

"Oh, dang. I didn't know all of that."

"Do you have a YouTube account?" Juan asked.

"No, what's that?" I replied sarcastically, with an over-the-top interest.

"It's this site where—"

"Juan, I know what YouTube is."

"Oh," he chuckled. "Well, you can listen to every Beatles song on there. Heck, you can listen to any song ever." He continued, "I like ones with a message. I don't think today's music has messages, though, except for Lady Gaga. She's a real artist and says meaningful stuff, you know. She uses her body as an art form."

"What? Lady Gaga?" I smirked at that. I heard her upbeat, overly sexual dance songs all the time at college parties.

"Yeah. I watched one of her videos the other day. It had over four hundred million views!"

"Dang. I'll have to listen to more of her music."

Juan looked around. Two teenagers sat at a table and stared at their phones. "Young people now don't know how to communicate in person. They're always on the computer or Facebook. They can't even figure out how to cross the street."

"Ha. I can't really argue with you on that one."

"But I have a Facebook account now too, though," he said. "I see some people who have a thousand 'friends'"—he used air quotes—"how can anyone have a thousand friends?" He rolled his eyes. "I mean *come on*! People try to add me, but if they don't have a picture, then no." He pounded his fist on the table.

Facebook had been a big part of my life in college. It was a party.

But I noticed my interest in it receding. Older people I knew started sending me friend requests. It was changing, becoming a mainstream forum where everyone communicated, not just young Americans—people like Juan were on it. It wasn't a bad thing. I'm sure it was exciting for older people reconnecting with friends and following their lives, but it was different than what I had grown used to. In general, I tended to side with Juan. I did believe that people around my age had an unhealthy addiction to screens and new social media. As someone who studied communication, the dynamics fascinated me—heck, writing a book about it is what I convinced my family and friends I was doing with my time instead of living homeless.

My eyelids grew heavy. I slept on and off the night before and couldn't find the energy to keep pushing my body. "I'mma take a nap, Juan. Keep a look out." I strategically propped my book, *The Picture of Dorian Gray*, in front of my face to fool any security guards.

"All right." Juan dug his nose into his Lennon biography.

My head shot up. "How much time did I sleep, Juan?" I demanded, too lazy to check my own watch.

Juan glanced at his wrist. "Five minutes."

"Whaaat?" My oily face convinced me I'd been asleep for hours. "I'm gonna go to the bathroom." I threw my book down and stomped toward the men's room by the elevators.

When I entered, a barefooted man in faded clothes with unkempt hair held his socks underneath the old blow-dryer. We greeted each other with a sup nod.

I stood in front of the sink and pounded my fist on the hot water knob. I cupped my hands, bent over, and splashed water on my face. The timer shut off quickly, so I repeated the motion three times to wipe away my grogginess.

"Do you have a razor?" the man asked.

I turned back and rubbed my wet beard. "Do you think I have one?" I joked. He belly-laughed, but it sounded hoarse and worn-down.

I reached for the door. "Have a good day, man," I said.

"Hey, you too. God bless!"

Interacting with other homeless individuals was common in public spaces. We detected each other's subtleties—our disheveled appearances, bags, and comfort performing activities in a room most people just *used*. We reached understanding without words. We smiled without judgment. I dried my socks below an air dryer before, and he splashed water on his face before too. We didn't need to imagine each other's struggles. We experienced it firsthand.

I began walking back to Juan.

"Rick!" a charismatic voice called.

"Huh?" I stopped and looked around. Julius approached me. "Oh, hey, Julius."

He put his hand on my shoulder. "What're you doin', man?"

"I'm sitting with Juan over there." I pointed to our table. "Come hang out with us."

Running into Julius wasn't a coincidence. At the library, running into people I knew or saw at Rawls was common. It was a hub for homeless individuals with its large space, computers, books, newspapers, magazines, and numerous other resources. It provided shelter from the elements too—like rain and snow or extreme hot and cold temperatures. The librarians were used to it. They never looked oddly at anyone. They carried themselves gracefully and empathized with their patrons, which made the homeless feel comfortable.

Juan looked up from his book, confused by the sudden noise from our movement. He looked over his shoulder and smiled. "Hey, Julius. What're you up to?"

"I was just on the computers. I'm trying to find another job." He had recently been laid off as a deliveryman. "Not gonna lie. I watched some porn too," he announced. "I can't get away with it on those Horizons computers."

Juan and I burst into laughter. The library computers had a screen covering the monitor. Only by sitting or standing directly in front of it could its contents be seen. Out of curiosity, I always walked the computer aisles once to count how many people watched porn. Usually three or four did. I tipped my theoretical hat to the unapologetic audacity it took to watch porn in a public setting. These people were comfortable in their own shoes and open.

"Rick here"—Juan pointed with his thumb—"just got some beauty rest."

"Yeah, 'cause those five minutes were *so* wonderful." I rolled my eyes.

"It's probably better than the sleep I got at O'Hare the other night," Julius said.

"Where'd you sleep at O'Hare?" I asked, having slept there before.

"Behind a column. When you get off the blue line there and go through the turnstile, you take a right. Close to there."

"Oh, I know where you're talking about. I've seen people behind those." I never slept behind them, personally. Sleeping out in the open like that made me too uncomfortable.

Julius raised his voice. "Yeah! I know you have. Every time I go there now, there's always someone in my spot." For such an unfortunate circumstance, Julius's widened eyes and animation made it funny, like delivering a punch line from a stand-up routine. I relished in his charismatic personality. He was easy to like. I wanted to go out of my way to help him.

"I've been going to O'Hare the last few Sundays," I said. "We're up so freakin' early at Rawls—the blue line is the only thing runnin'. I fall asleep on the train and wake up at the airport. Then, I go to Terminal 3 because it has the dimmest lights," I explained with my hands. "I sleep on those chairs for half an hour, then go to Terminal 2 to buy coffee and watch the political shows for the week. And then before I go back to Horizons, I go to Terminal 1 to people watch. It's the most active."

Juan and Julius nodded their heads with keen interest. "Really?" Julius asked. He scratched his forearm. I remembered he complained about his sensitive skin before.

"Yeah. Along the way to each terminal, I memorize flights in case security confronts me. It hasn't happened yet, though."

"You're a paranoid person, Rick," Juan joked.

"That's actually a good idea," Julius said, rubbing his chin. "I might need to try that."

"Just don't do it on Sunday morning. That's my thing," I teased. "But if you're looking for some better sleep at O'Hare, try the bus depot. The elevator is right over there by those columns."

"Okay." Julius confirmed with a head bob. "What's that like?" he asked.

"It's weird," I admitted, "but at least you're not gonna to have to sleep on the hard floor. There's these cushions. I don't really know how to explain it well"—I contorted my face—"large plants are in the center of 'em in a circle. It was hard for me not to fall off—and you're bigger so it might be even worse." I threw my hands up. "I don't know. Try it out, I guess."

His cheeks shined. My inability to describe my experience amused him.

"Anyway, guys, I gotta run. I gotta get back to Horizons," I said. "You wanna come with me, Julius?"

"Nah. I'm gonna go straight to Rawls," he said.

"Cool. I'll see you guys there later then." I stood up and packed my book into my backpack. "Oh, Juan! I forgot to ask you." I swung my backpack around my shoulder. "You goin' to the bar with Vinny for the Bears game?"

"Why? You worried about listening to him for three hours by yourself?" Juan teased.

I pointed my finger at him. "That's *exactly* what I'm worried about."

"Well, don't worry. I'll be there."

Journal Entry — October 1, 2011

I'm approaching the two-month mark living homeless. It's strange. This whole week, I felt relaxed and comfortable in the shelter. I don't feel like "the new guy" anymore. In fact, new guys come up to me and ask questions about the shelter process and homelessness in general—and I can answer them! So far, I've had goals for each month. The first month was to sleep outside and eat in soup kitchens to understand how that felt. This second month was to stay in a shelter program and make friends. And I did that.

I'm somebody here. I feel like I belong. People know who I am. I can't go anywhere without people saying, "Hey, Rick!" or giving me a sup nod. It's not everyone, or even a large amount, but it's enough. I have friends at Inspired Horizons but more at Rawls. I'm not afraid to show off my personality, either.

I am, however, worried about when I'm alone without my friends. I don't do so hot. I get down, in these depressive, negative moods. I fucking hate the routine of everything. Each day feels like the previous. It's purgatory. Once I'm with my friends, I'm more positive and time passes normally instead of being trapped in some warped dimension. When something bad comes up, they help me laugh through it.

I don't know what my goal is for the third month. To be honest, I'm reaching my overall goal quicker than I originally thought. I think I'm about 70 percent there but have no idea where the last 30 percent comes from. I'm going to keep doing what I'm doing. I'll continue staying at Rawls. Maybe I'll figure it out.

CHAPTER FOURTEEN

THE PLANE CRASHED

"Over here, Rick!" Vinny called across the bar, waving his arms from a high-top table in front of a projection screen. Only two other tables had people. It was quiet and dark inside, compared to the sunlight and increasingly active intersection outside. Sundays in Chicago didn't move much until late morning. It felt strange to enter a bar while homeless—and not just to use its bathroom. My stomach danced just thinking about it, not knowing what to expect. Would people know we were homeless? Would we be treated differently?

I meandered over and joined Vinny, his dad, and Juan.

"What's up?" I took a seat next to Vinny. He wore a gray T-shirt with the Chicago Bears logo on it. His hair was slicked back. *He must've used half a container of hair gel on that.*

"Me and my dad got here a half hour ago to grab this spot." Vinny tapped the table. "Did you walk past Wrigley Field to get here?"

"Yeah," I replied. "How could I miss it? It's right off the red line stop."

"It's awesome, isn't it? Did you know the Cubs have the most fans in America?"

"How do you figure that?" I asked.

Vinny dismissed me. "It's a fact. You know what we call *your* stadium?" He didn't allow me any time to respond. He tilted his chin high into the air. "Wrigley North! Because Chicago fans go up to Milwaukee and fill it up."

I rolled my eyes, cocking my head. "When was the last time the Cubs won the World Series?"

"1908," Vinny said solemnly. Juan watched with a smirk. "But they're going to be really good in a few years," Vinny quipped. "They just hired that GM from Boston. They won two titles with him—just watch!"

"All right. We'll see," I mocked.

The Bears game kicked off on the screen. The bar was quickly filling up. People dressed in navy-blue and orange Bears clothes joined their friends at tables. Of course, a few nonconformists wore sky-blue jerseys, supporting the Carolina Panthers. The bar grew louder with background chatter and shuffling. An excited energy replaced the sleepiness inside the bar when I arrived.

I wondered whether it was a common thing for other homeless individuals to go to a bar and spend money on food. Were we an anomaly? I wouldn't have come if Vinny weren't paying for me. I was conservative with my money. I didn't know where Vinny got his money from. It wasn't any of my business. Then again, we came to escape the homeless environment and eat a good meal. It was more of a one-off rather than a consistent routine.

"I think the Bears will win by ten," Vinny said. Vinny's dad nodded. His dark eyebrows looked stern. He had confidence in his son's prediction. "What do you think, Juan?"

"Oh, I don't know. I don't know much about football. Maybe the Bears will win by four?"

"Rick?" Vinny asked.

"The Bears will lose by five."

Vinny's eyebrows pinched together. "What? The Panthers have a rookie quarterback. They're not going to win."

I shrugged. "I guess we'll see."

The bar was full. The server came by and took our orders. Under the impression Vinny would pay for my food, I splurged on a *grass-fed* burger with a pretzel bun and fancy-sounding ingredients and—of course—I substituted tater tots in place of fries for a dollar more. Vinny huddled over his father, explaining what each item was.

"No, Dad. You won't like that." He pointed to the menu. He lost his patience. "My dad will just have the chicken sandwich," Vinny told the server.

"I don't want that!" his dad snapped back with lowered eyebrows.

"Too bad. That's what we're ordering," Vinny scolded. The server flashed an awkward look at Juan and me.

Watching the game at a bar made me feel uncomfortable. The normalcy of it gave me a knot of unease—almost paranoia. The four of us were homeless, but no one knew. I constantly swiveled my head, checking to see if other tables stared at us but noticed nothing. Feeling embarrassed scared me so much that I overcompensated by maintaining a confident, erect posture the whole game.

Our time at the bar should have been relaxing, but I didn't enjoy it. I overthought the idea of *homeless*, like other guys in the shelter. Society's looming idea of homelessness affected me too. I worried about feeling unwelcomed because of a conjured label in my head.

"I bet Devin Hester will run this back," Vinny broadcasted.

"Think so?" Juan asked, adjusting his hat.

The Chicago punt returner caught the ball and streaked in between two Carolina players' arms.

"Here we go!" Vinny yelled, vice-gripping my arm.

Hester streaked across midfield, dashing to the end zone. The whole bar erupted in applause and cheers. A raucous Vinny sprang from his seat and high-fived everyone in the vicinity.

"I told you, Rick!" He pointed in my face. "I told you he'd return it!"

I shrugged again. "You *did* call it."

The Bears won by five points, and Vinny flashed his shirt at me repeatedly with a cocky smile. As big of a fan as Vinny was, I believed the real reason Vinny was so adamant about watching the game together was because he needed a moment with other people besides his dad. The responsibility of looking after him nonstop frustrated him.

"Thanks again for the meal, Vinny." I patted him on the back. "See you guys later. I gotta get to Horizons."

"See ya, Rick." They waved goodbye and watched me walk away.

"Rick, where were you all day?" Pete asked, lying in front of the TV, using an old strip of carpet padding as a pillow. The dayroom was packed.

"What do you mean? I was here before dinner."

"Oh, you were? I guess I didn't see you."

"Maybe it was earlier. I went to a bar in Wrigleyville to watch the Bears game with Vinny, his dad, and Juan."

"Oh! How'd that go?" he asked.

"About what you'd expect watching a Bears game with Vinny," I joked. He nodded in amusement. "The food was a lot better than the frozen ham we just had at dinner." I rolled my eyes.

He chuckled. "You didn't like it?" he asked with a sarcastic smile.

I grimaced. "Not particularly."

We watched the football game on TV. I found myself sunken, feeling blue, without a specific trigger event. I plugged right back into the soul-crushing routine. Nothing provided relief. Escaping the shelter environment didn't help. I didn't experience pure fun and bliss at the bar like I had hoped. I was uncomfortable. There was a constant fog that followed me wherever I went.

"Whew boy, that Rodgers is a beast!" someone shouted, interrupting my momentary reflection. Aaron Rodgers threw a touchdown pass, continuing the annihilation of the Broncos.

"The Packers are toying with these guys. Don't mess with the champs!" another guy yelled.

An unwritten rule existed in the dayroom: only football shall play on TV on Sundays. Guys took a big risk by ditching their chair, even if they left a bag to save it. The dayroom was full on those days.

Pete turned around to me again. "Look at this, Rick." He showed me his hand. It was swollen and purple.

"Whoa! What the hell happened?" I leaned closer and squinted to get a better look at his wound.

"Got bit by a pit bull yesterday. I was trying to get back into my house. My ex-wife guards it pretty well." A sardonic laugh escaped his mouth.

"Damn. You gonna get that checked out?"

"Nah. It'll be fine." He pulled his hand away from me. "I have some medication too." He patted his backpack and smiled.

"Whew. All right, man. Good luck." I shook my head. Pete was one tough dude. If I had gotten bit like that, I'd cry for my mom and ask to be rushed to the hospital. Not Pete. From what he told me, he and his ex-wife had issues. He wanted a divorce, and she refused for years to sign it. He said she's crazy and overdramatic.

I glanced at the clock above the TV. The van hadn't arrived yet. Seven o'clock passed. The guys who stayed at the Gym gradually disappeared. Being late to Rawls didn't bother me *too much*—we didn't have to wait outside in the cold then. And guys didn't stare at us when the *hobo-express* (I learned it had been nicknamed) parked in front of the building. Some of the west-side guys didn't like us north-siders staying there. The contract between Rawls and Inspired Horizons was poorly communicated.

Every fifteen minutes, staff members repeatedly told us Phil was on his way. He grew more inconsistent over the last week, but this was abnormal, even for him.

The clock struck eight, and still no sign of Phil.

"We gotta shut the dayroom down. Bring your things to the cafeteria and wait there," a staff member instructed.

Pete and I exchanged odd glances and then followed orders.

We waited in the cafeteria. Six of us sat at one table; five others scattered to their own. Marquis set out crackers for anyone who was hungry.

"I think Phil's on drugs, guys," someone said. "He's been sayin' some weird shit lately and hasn't shown up on time." Another guy nodded his head.

"Phil don't smoke no pipe, man!" Reggie said, denying the accusation. "Phil don't smoke no pipe!"

"I don't know, Reggie," Marquis chimed in. "He's never been this late."

"I'm tellin' you. It ain't that!" Reggie reinforced.

"Well, something is going on that we don't know about. Something different than usual," I said.

Pete nodded at me. "Right."

I didn't know what happened. Drugs could have been the issue. It wasn't unreasonable to believe, but I refused to support it in front of Reggie. Other explanations needed consideration and, of course, it was natural to speculate—the staff didn't provide any information. We didn't hear from them again. Communication was cut off.

"All right, guys." Reggie stood up. "The plane crashed and we're in this together!" He inspired us with his analogy and aggressive waving of his arms. He was like a hall-of-fame basketball coach, beloved politician, and military general all rolled into one. We each smiled. Reggie's enthusiasm lightened the mood. We swallowed our fate easier. Going to Rawls was no longer an option.

Reggie dashed to another table. "What we gotta do is put together these chairs to make a nice bed for ourselves." He started reaching for chairs to demonstrate for us.

"Reggie can't stand not having the attention," Marquis teased.

"What! I bet you five whole dollars I can be quiet," Reggie declared.

Pete laughed and nudged me. "Oh, I'll take that bet."

"All you guys think I can't be quiet, hey?" He slapped the table. "Slick Rick, what about you?"

I snorted. "I'm gonna take that bet too."

"That's a shame. Y'all don't believe in me. All right." He pushed up his hat. "When do we start?"

Marquis laughed. "We already started."

"Aww, shoot! Y'all hustled me." Reggie spun in a circle and slapped the table again. "I ain't givin' no five dollars! Believe that!" We burst into laughter as Reggie stomped to the bathroom.

"He does have a point about the beds, though," Pete admitted, looking around the cafeteria.

"Yeah, he does." Marquis sighed. "Just don't tell him that."

I stood up and announced, "Well, I'm gonna get ready for bed." I dug for my toothbrush in my backpack and sauntered to the bathroom.

Reggie was standing in front of the mirror when I entered. He turned to me. "Rick, put this in your hair. You'll get all the bitches!" Reggie shoved a container of Axe hair gel in my face.

I leaned back then grabbed it. I twisted off the cap and sniffed it, wincing at the potent smell. "Where'd you get this?"

"Pretty white girl gave it to me downtown. I can't use it. It's for white people."

I smirked. "Uh, thanks."

"No problem. I'm a generous man. Goes back to my GD days."

"Your what?"

"I was a Gangster Disciple. Grew up in the Robert Taylor projects—the largest project in America." He was both proud and weary. "Shoot, I can't even tell you some of the shit that went on. Those buildings are long gone now, but those memories will never disappear. Ain't nothin' like it." He stared into the mirror.

I backed away, avoiding the likeliness I'd hear something I couldn't unhear. "You know what"—I pointed to the door with my thumb—"I'm gonna wait to brush my teeth. I think I'm gonna eat some of those crackers Marquis had."

I didn't think it was Reggie's first time experiencing homelessness. For the most part, I thought he handled it as well as anyone could. He seemed to be in good spirits around others. The company of friends energized him. I related to that. However, I always wondered about his dark, silent moments. Did living homeless—and the pressure that came with that—bring out bad memories and traumatic events? Homelessness removed one of the basic needs of life. It created stress from what should be simplicities of the day. Struggling to meet those made someone reflect on their own life, their worth, and value to others. Darkness knocked on the door. It exaggerated one's inner insecurities. I wanted to be there for Reggie if he needed me. But I also wanted to give him space and privacy. I cared about him and wanted him to persevere.

CHAPTER FIFTEEN

WALKING THE TIGHTROPE OF PASSIVENESS

I lumbered through the cafeteria and sat across Elias. I struggled to shake the grogginess from hardly being able to sleep the previous night. Volunteers kicked us out at six thirty, so we trudged across the alleyway and waited till seven in the dayroom, which irritated me. We were misled by staff members and slept in the cafeteria, but they couldn't let us just stay until breakfast?

"You slept where?" Elias hollered.

"Yup." I nodded.

Elias shook his head. "That's awful."

"Eh. It is what it is." His jaw still hung open, but I only shrugged. "At least it broke up the routine a bit."

"How did you sleep?"

"Not well," I answered. *Not well* was generous. It was terrible. "First, I put some of these chairs together"—I pointed to the empty ones next to us—"but the problem wasn't really lying on them, though. It was that they're all different." Some chairs were taller than others; some chairs had soft cushioning while others didn't; some chairs wobbled while others balanced. No uniformity existed. Inspired Horizons took what it could get.

Elias leaned back. "Ohhhh. That's too bad."

"I gave up halfway through the night. I just slept on the floor underneath a table. Don't you wish you still went to Rawls?" I joked.

Elias shrugged apathetically. "The apartments aren't much better upstairs. They're better than Rawls, of course, but they have their own problems."

"Like what?" I asked.

"Well, I have three roommates. One smells like cigarette butts that laid out in the rain for a week. He watches movies every night on this small DVD player." Elias shook his head. "And he makes these noises with his mouth when he chews." Elias pursed his lips together and made obnoxious kissing sounds over and over. *Pah! Pah! Pah!* "It drives me nuts!"

"That sucks. Did you tell him to stop?"

"That's the thing, though. It's a delicate situation because if I get him mad, I'm afraid he's going to steal my stuff." Elias frowned. "I'm already missing two bars of soap."

"That doesn't seem like you, though. I've seen you put your foot down before." There was a time when a woman tried to take his chair at breakfast. He erupted like a volcano. His face burned red, and I swore I could see heat waves emitting from his long-haired head.

"I know. It's *not* like me. But things get complicated when you're living in the same room as someone."

"Yeah, true." Elias was still homeless and still had to endure the same problems like the people at Rawls. His particular living situation had improved and become more stable, but he wasn't out of the woods yet. He still balanced on a tightrope of passiveness, not wanting to upset others, worried about escalation and retaliation. I knew how hard he worked to find more opportunities. I hoped it'd pay off for him soon.

"Oh, that's not all, though. My other roommate scratches himself like crazy. He folds his clothes on this crate, so I looked closer at it and tiny bugs were crawling all over." He raised his eyebrows, ducked his head under the table, and rummaged through his bag. "So I bought this." He whipped out a bottle of bed bug spray like an infomercial.

I barreled over with laughter.

The topic of bed bugs often barged its way into conversations. Guys discussed it like an ongoing war. They revealed battle wounds; they warned where the enemy hid; and they advised which weapons killed best. I had been fortunate in that I had mostly avoided conflicts. To my knowledge, I suffered two bite marks. Andre had been letting me choose my bed, but one night, I let my guard down, signing in fourth. Andre was in a ferocious mood from people repeatedly disobeying the rules, including an argument with Armando about sneaking outside to smoke a cigarette. He didn't let anyone choose their bed, sending me straight to the front line. I deployed the tactic of dragging my mat a foot away from the wall, perhaps limiting the bed bugs' accessibility. It proved effective, and I encouraged others to do the same.

Pete approached our table. He threw his backpack on an empty chair and the *Red Eye* on the table. He sat down and scrambled through it for the Sudoku puzzle but landed on the horoscopes.

"What's your sign, Rick?" he asked, studying the page.

"Capricorn."

He cleared his throat. "You're going insane. You're stressed out, and your partner should be aware."

"Yeah, maybe it's 'cause I'm fuckin' homeless, and I slept on the floor last night!"

Pete burst into laughter. "That was a good call, though—to sleep on the floor instead of the chairs." He smiled. "Didn't mess up your back as much."

"It was." I rolled my eyes, grinning.

Elias shook his head with raised eyebrows. "Well, I'm glad I wasn't with you guys last night." He slowly stood up. "I have to go to a few places today. It was nice seeing you both." He grabbed his tray and started for the trash can, waving goodbye.

I looked at the table next to us. A young mother gathered her two rambunctious kids. She strapped their colorful plastic backpacks around their shoulders for school. She hurried them along, but her daughter wanted to gulp the last bit of her Kool-Aid. The mother repeatedly tapped the table.

Pete looked at me. "Why aren't you working on the puzzle?"

"You know why. I do it later before roll call or at Rawls. It gives me something to look forward to."

"Oh. Right. I knew that." Pete laughed. "I haven't taken my meds yet—that's why I won't shut up. There's eleven of 'em—mainly painkillers but some antipsychotics too." My eyebrows shot up. I didn't know he took so many pills. I didn't even know where he got them. Maybe the VA? That'd explain Pete, but I wasn't quite as sure as the other homeless individuals I saw with pills. "I'm probably crazy because my dad beat me. He'd yell, 'Are you crying? I'll give you something to cry about!'" Pete waved his clenched fist. I tried to imagine what growing up in an environment with a parent like that would be like. I was glad my dad was never like that.

He continued, "A lot of times, I don't feel pain. When I had a gash or something, I'd stitch it up myself. People asked, 'Doesn't that hurt?' And then, I'd poke myself all over my arm with the needle and say, 'Nope!'" A smile crept along his face, only to disappear when he said, "It sure helped me in the SEALs, though."

"I bet the SEALs are all freakin' huge, hey?" I asked.

"No." He shook his head, his peppered hair flopping around. "But you have to be super athletic. They're more around my size to blend in. We carry an attitude that requires us to be killed twice. We'd go into cities, assassinate twenty-one people, and then leave. The marines get the credit." He dipped his head condescendingly. "But that's how we like it. No one knows about us." I tilted my head and shifted my body in the squeaky chair. "It's some crazy stuff, though. One guy stabbed me in my guts, but I didn't realize it until later." He lifted up his shirt and showed me his scar. "I hit him forty-three times with an icepick. One time, I got shot in the leg and had a hole this big." He made a circle with his thumb and index fingers.

"Dang." I put my elbows on the table and leaned closer. I listened with my mouth agape. The sacrifices Pete and other Americans in the military made were unbelievable to me.

"I thought it was weird how sometimes I heard on the news that eighteen out of twenty-three Navy SEALs died in a certain place. You always see a team of five to seven people—no more, no less. We don't want it any other way. You have to be stealthy and move quickly. Rule number one is don't put multiple teams in the same place since SEALs are so valuable. Over three thousand guys enter boot camp for six months. Ninety-four move on, and only twelve graduate—enough for two teams. I tied the obstacle course record during my boot camp. My instructor was the one who held it, but he cheered me on to beat it anyway. I tried four times but could never break it." He slapped the table, and I jumped back from the noise.

He hung his head. "I'm the only one left from my team. Man, we did some crazy things." It had to be difficult knowing your closest friends had all died. It'd probably send me into an existential crisis, wondering why I was the only one to survive. That required a particular toughness—not like what Pete had described, but a deeper thoughtfulness. He possessed that too but wouldn't let it on. He hid it from others, but I could see through it.

"In the Philippines, we'd go diving. We each had a bunch of flags and, for fun, we'd see who could stick the most flags on one shark. They're usually sand sharks—a little bigger than three feet, but they could still rip your arm or leg off," he explained. My smiling mouth hung open. "One time, my buddy tried to stick his flag in the shark's dorsal fin, but it swam in a circle and bit him in the ass! What was even funnier was that he was wearing a wetsuit so the shark couldn't release its grip. So here we were on this boat, using harpoons to hit this waggling shark stuck to my friend's ass." Pete leaned back, slapping the table. "God, that was hilarious!" He grinned enormously. "He had to get around one hundred seventy stiches, though."

"No way! Really?" Sharks scared me, and Pete and his friends actively harassed one. He was a special breed of man.

The cafeteria had almost cleared out. It was quieter around us, and our conversation seemed to echo.

"We'd get drunk—like really, really drunk. We each had our own bottle of tequila, and we'd go cave diving. We'd be gagging the whole time." Pete's tongue dangled from his mouth. He sighed. "I miss them. But you know what you sign up for."

"Excuse me, gentlemen," a female staff member interjected, grabbing our trays. "The cafeteria is closed."

Pete inspired me. His life was rich. He lived it to the fullest, which is more than most people could say. What society considered flaws, he turned into a career—a career that helped ensure others could dream. He embodied the spirit of America. He owned up to the choices he made and protected the freedom to make those choices. He displayed exhaustion and struggle, but never regret or bitterness. Pete strengthened my desire for humility.

———————

I blew a cloud of smoke in the air, staring at the garage's deteriorating ceiling.

Max ambled through the open garage door and approached my old patio table. His eyes barely opened.

He put his hand on the edge of the surface, and the table screeched across the brick ground. "Oh, sorry," he slurred. He bent down to my ear and whispered, "Take a walk with me." I barely made out his words.

I waved him away from my personal space. "Nah, I'm good here, man."

"All right. Well, last night at the Gym," Max mumbled, "I took these pills to help me relax, but I took five and overdosed." He leaned back and tried widening his almost-shut eyes. "I was knocked out and gravity was a whole lot different. Other guys told me to hide and go to sleep so I didn't get kicked out." He bent down to my ear again. "I have a bunch of extras. You interested in taking them?" he garbled. I didn't know if the heating sensation inside me was from anger or social discomfort.

"I'm good for now, but I'll let you know if anything changes," I said.

Max pointed out my new habits before, but his disturbed me. This was the first time I'd seen him this bad. He was a sharp guy. I figured he'd quickly get back on track, but I was wrong. The stress swallowed him. Homelessness became too much for him. It could do that to someone and didn't require a lot of time. Homelessness affected people in many ways, especially mental health. I knew my own had slipped. It was a topic society avoided. As Americans, we'd been ingrained to be tough and act like superheroes. As a man, discussing feelings with others was a sign of weakness. Most of my life, I hid my emotions. I bought into that narrative and, instead, bottled everything up inside. At some point, it would be too much to handle. It hurt me to see Max that way, but I felt betrayed that he encouraged me to join him.

Max stumbled toward the dayroom. He crossed paths with Clyde, who joined me at the table.

"I didn't know you smoked, Rick," Clyde said with a stiff face.

I shook off my disorientation from Max. "Yeah, usually I smoke waiting for the van. Luis gives 'em to me." I pointed to Luis, standing in the corner, talking to someone.

Clyde lit a grape cigarillo. "You want one—for when that's done?" He pointed to the cigarette in my left hand, which was almost to the filter.

"Sure." I reached across my body, and Clyde handed me a new one.

Clyde puffed smoke from his mouth. "I met this nice female cop when I was scrappin' today," he stated with revelation. I leaned closer to distinguish his tired inflections. "I thought she was gonna get me in trouble. You're not supposed to be goin' into areas, pullin' metal and all. Instead, she's pointin' out pieces I should pick. That's never happened to me."

I tilted my head and pushed up my glasses. "Yeah?"

"If you don't have a fence up, or say it's private property, then people will go after the metal. You have to get up real early so you can get scraps before others. I'll probably get up at like three or four o'clock to get a jump on the day. A lot of times, you can get six to eight hundred pounds in a buggie—one of those small carts." He demonstrated with his arms.

"Eight hundred pounds!" My head jerked forward. He remained stone-faced and reached to his forehead to adjust his yellow bandana.

"Yeah. It all depends on how good you get at handling and steering. You gotta get used to it, but it's possible. You can get like ten cents per pound, so that's like sixty bucks. I store my cart by the place I do crack. I know people who stay over there, and they'll look after it," he said. "I can't just sit around and watch TV and smoke and do nothing like these other guys here. At least I'm out working." He tapped the table. "I'm not even beggin'. I have more worth, you know—like I'm accomplishing somethin'." He turned his body to me. "You don't have any habits, so you could do well."

"Yeah, I guess I could." I looked thoughtfully to the ceiling. "Maybe."

"I was the same as you nine months ago. I was outta jail and at one of them warm spots in the city. I saw guys in there drinking and stuff. 'How do they get the money to do that?' I thought. That's when I learned about scrappin'. I gave it a try, and it worked for me."

"Hmm." I admired Clyde; he was an enterprising man. Most people stumble upon ideas but never act on them. He was a man of action.

Clyde shook his head. "Some people are shitty, though. I'll go past people's yards on the south side 'cause they got junk layin' all around." He scanned the garage with his arm. "I'll ask them if I can take some, but they just say no. They aren't ever gonna use any of it. They just try to make it harder for other people." The veins in his forearms looked ready to pop out of his skin.

I knew exactly what he meant. Some people had such a negative perspective on life that they wanted to drag others down with them. They focused on their problems and created new ones for other people.

He continued, "Some places put yellow caution tape around a scrap area. They don't want people goin' in."

The irony of putting caution tape in a forbidden area humored me. I stood up from my chair and altered my voice to sound like a game show host. "Ladies and gentlemen, you can go in here for metal"—I showcased with my arm—"but *please* be careful!"

Clyde's hard exterior vanished momentarily. He broke so hard into laughter that he lost his balance and fell to the ground. The metal chair screeched. It must've been a long time since he laughed. It was like he forgot how to laugh. For a few seconds, it was like watching a child enjoy the blissfulness of life, unrestrained by the boundaries adults created to be more serious. Guys looked toward us, distracted by the sudden noise. They smiled after the initial confusion.

My hands tingled. My weightless body collapsed back onto my chair—not from exhaustion, but from fulfillment. I smiled with both satisfaction and wonder.

———

"What the hell happened to your arm?" I asked Juan. We sat next to each other in the shower line. Parliament's "Flashlight" played from the stereo behind us.

"I got a shot," he replied with a frown. I squinted at his bruised bicep. He wore a plain white T-shirt. Sleeves usually covered his arms.

"Is that supposed to happen?" I asked.

"Of course not," he said. "I don't know. I think it's because I'm getting old."

I smirked. "*Getting* old?"

Juan laughed. "Fine. I *am* old."

"Is it true a person loses half an inch in height when aging? 'Cause I don't have much to work with." I laughed.

"I don't know"—he patted his bald head—"but my feet grew bigger." He swung his feet from under his chair. "I've had problems with my feet for a while now."

"Aside from your ankle problem?" I asked.

"Yeah. It's because they're flat. People with flat feet have more problems," he assured me as if he were a doctor. He placed his ankle on his knee and pointed to the surface of his foot. "See how I have no arches?"

"Mhm." Juan looked down at my flip-flops.

"Rick, be cautious!" He warned with his finger. "Go to a podiatrist and see if there is anything you can do. Take care of your feet now because you could have troubles later."

"All right, all right." I waved. "What else do I need to know about getting old?"

"Keep a good posture." Juan stood up. "Don't walk with your head looking down because, eventually, you'll fall on your face," he warned. "And help your body by eating healthy and exercising— even though a lot comes from heredity." I nodded my head with a studious gaze. He sat back down in the shower line.

I became distracted momentarily once again. A handful of middle-aged women walked around the tables and handed out flyers. A nearby clinic sponsored free STD testing. While a health clinic came to Rawls every Monday and Thursday, more resources were always welcomed.

The vibe inside the room was different than usual; it was warmer. The women provided serenity. Each night, fifty to seventy-five men surrounded each other. I looked around and postures were straightened. An aura of politeness came over the room. It was relieving. "Thank you, ma'am" could be heard repeatedly. Perhaps the motherly presence assured the men everything would be all right.

I turned back to Juan. "I bet you'd probably be in even better shape if you weren't homeless," I said. "You look like you're still in pretty good shape to me."

He sighed. "Yeah. I think so too. Thank God for the VA, or I'd be screwed." Juan served in the US Air Force and attended the academy. He was a bright individual.

Learning more about their backgrounds dispelled my previous conception about education levels among the homeless. Some men had college degrees. Pete had a degree in anthropology and geography from the University of Washington. Though it lowered the likeliness of homelessness, it didn't grant immunity.

"Oh, you know what else?" Juan said, remembering something. "You keep losing your energy too."

"I need one for the showers," Keon yelled from outside the shower room. I rose from my chair and leaned toward Juan.

"I don't know if you know this, Juan, but I'm going to be twenty-two forever." I stuck my tongue out at Juan. I leaned back with my tongue sticking out from my mouth and walked toward Keon.

Almost everyone sat in their chairs against the kitchen wall. Volunteers began folding up tables.

"You guys want mine?" I asked Reggie and Marquis, pointing to my plate of cut-up turkey slices resting in rice and beans. They waved me off.

"Shorty, Shorty! Over here!" A large man waved aggressively, twenty feet away. I swung my head. "I'll take your plate!"

Reggie and Marquis shot up from their chairs with their bodies coiled. The term Shorty was demeaning and disrespectful. They stared at him with stern eyes and wrinkled noses. I stood frozen, lowering my eyebrows toward the obnoxious man. I twisted my head at the man and then back at Reggie and Marquis, confused as to what to do. *Why throw food away if someone was still hungry?*

I crept to the man and handed him my tray. He didn't stand up to greet me or give me eye contact. He threw a meaningless thank-you to my face. I felt my heart race, like it had just received a shot of adrenaline. My teeth ground together. My face tightened trying to restrain my rage.

I returned to Reggie and Marquis with my hands on my hips. Marquis stared at me through his glasses.

Reggie fumed from his ears. "Rick, you know we got your back. Any of these dudes in here try to mess with you, I'm gonna go off on 'em!" He raised his clenched fists.

"Maybe another night, Reggie. I appreciate it, though." I turned back to the ungrateful individual with narrowed eyes.

Like Elias, I walked my own tightrope of passiveness. Homelessness stripped a man of many things, but in the shelter, they clung to pride and ego. At times, it seemed more emboldened. I wasn't excluded. I had my own ego I tried to protect. Reggie and Marquis knew right away that the man's comments were a blow to it. As my friends, they were willing to stand up for me. My mind wrestled: fight or flight? I'd chosen flight in almost every situation at the shelter. That was the appropriate response. Around Armando, whom I hadn't seen in a while, I especially experienced the fight or flight feeling. I didn't want to create enemies who would threaten the security of my belongings or myself. I didn't want to get involved in a scuffle either, which could result in being barred from the shelter temporarily. Each time felt like a test. Wounded pride made a man do foolish things, ultimately against his own interests.

CHAPTER SIXTEEN

I PUT YOU IN THAT SELECT GROUP

I joined Vinny and Juan at our table. Many times, we sat at the table next to the shower line; we could keep a better eye on our stuff while we sat in the row of chairs. I stared down at my plate of mystery meat and sulked. Juan nudged me.

"Look up there." He pointed to pink, blue, and green balloons stuck to the high ceiling. We didn't know how long they'd been there—or how long they'd remain. Children must've been playing some time before the shelter opened. What a juxtaposition. Balloons were colorful and symbolized happiness. They contrasted the manila-colored ceiling and wobbling rusted fans. Children only wanted to have fun. They were innocent. Perhaps hours later, grown men experiencing homelessness replaced them. They didn't have their whole lives ahead of them like the kids. But it was like the kids purposely left them there, to wink at us and to remind us to smile—to remember the small things in life that can bring joy and bliss.

Suddenly, I felt a tap on my shoulder.

"Hey, Rick. You got a minute?" Andre asked.

"Uh, sure," I said. I stood up and followed Andre to an empty table. I sat down gingerly, preparing for an uncomfortable conversation.

"How old are you?" Andre asked, teetering between casual and professional.

"Twenty-two," I answered.

His head shot forward. "Twenty-two?" he repeated. I had assumed he already knew. He could've just looked at my intake form.

I proactively explained my situation. "My mother and I don't get along too great and, well, she sort of kicked me out one day. I think she'll have me back around the holidays so until then, I'm kind of just holding out."

"What're you doin' for money in the meantime?" he asked. I broke eye contact for a brief moment. Telling him I memorized my checking account number and withdrew a little money each week seemed weird and too confusing to explain. I reached for answers inside my head but couldn't grasp any. Instead, I gave a vague reply.

"Well, being in this whole situation, I got to thinking I should go back to school. I don't want to live paycheck to paycheck. I figure getting an education would be the best way for that."

He scowled at me. "Well, you gotta do somethin'!" His reaction seared into my brain. My stomach knotted; I wished I could take back my words. Everyone at Rawls lived paycheck to paycheck, including Andre. *Who the hell am I to say that?*

Andre broke the silence by sharing more about himself. "I'm originally from Virginia. I had a girlfriend but lost my job as a painter. Turns out people can stomach an ugly wall when money's tight." He flashed a reassuring smile and I stared at the gap between his teeth.

His story seemed to mirror others I had heard. America was hit hard from the 2008 financial crisis; it threw many lives into turmoil. I was in college during the worst part. Friends of mine who graduated relayed back to me how challenging it was to find a job. Companies struggled and couldn't keep all their employees. People had been let go and, in turn, recent college graduates looking for entry-level jobs competed against others with twice the experience. I saw the effect of the crisis most during my summer job, installing carpeting for my neighbor's installation company. Newly built houses were rare; instead, people replaced a room's carpet here or there. Similar to what Andre said, people could stomach old and ugly carpet when money was tight.

Andre continued, "I came to Chicago and stayed in a shelter too. I stayed at one on the south side and a different one here on the west side. Some guys in here"—he looked around the room—"use Rawls as a safe haven and shelter. They make a life of it. Others have what it takes to move on from their situation. I put you in that select group." He pointed at my chest. "Go down to the Department of Human Services at ten South Kedzie. Find Benella and tell her Andre sent you."

"Okay." I nodded and locked eyes with Andre.

He leaned toward me. "You don't have a record, do you?" he asked.

"No." I shook my head.

"That's good!" He smiled and bounced in his chair. "You can get your own place for three months free. If your situation gets better, just hand over the key and leave. Poof." He flung his hands. "If it doesn't get better, you can stay there for like three hundred dollars a month. While you're there, you can look for a job and get back on your feet."

"Okay," I muttered.

Andre stiffened his posture and stared at me with a demanding face. "You don't want to keep coming to Rawls, traveling during the day and puttin' up with all the stuff here. I told you some information to help you, but if you keep staying here, that's on you." He pointed at my chest again. He stood up from his chair and gave me a quick nod.

Well, shit. I lost my appetite. I remained alone at the table, brooding from the conversation. Andre spoon-fed me a strategy to leave Rawls, but I planned to stay for at least another month. *Would I appear ungrateful if I ignored his information? Is he going to treat me differently now?* My heart ached, like it shrank inside me. I looked up to Andre and didn't want our relationship to deteriorate.

CHAPTER SEVENTEEN

THE MOST INTERESTING MAN IN THE WORLD

The Inspired Horizons free store opened at 9:00 a.m. It was a large room filled with donated clothes. It opened only on Friday, and only for a few hours. People could take whatever they needed.

Clyde and I waited together in the crowded stairwell. His yellow bandana was cockeyed. I glanced at my watch; it was 8:45. Conversations and coughs echoed off the walls. Shuffling feet rustled. My heavy backpack was on the dirty floor. I casually leaned against the wall and looked at Clyde. His beady eyes told me something was on his mind.

"There're so many rotten people here," he mumbled.

"Why do you say that?" I asked.

"People just always want somethin'. You know? Somethin's always attached. Like the other night, I was talking with Dante. We thought we might make more money if we worked together scrappin', but he was puttin' all these stipulations on it and stuff."

"Oh." I exaggerated one of my dimples and shifted my weight to the other leg. I spoke to Dante before at Rawls and got along with him well. I started raising my hand, as if about to convince Clyde that he probably misinterpreted Dante, but realized it was a dumb idea. Clyde wouldn't have changed his mind.

"Or like Elias," Clyde continued. "He asked me for some laundry detergent and that if I helped him, he'd 'rock my world.'" Clyde's face didn't move. His tired eyes showed a history of failed relationships. He seemed to mistrust everyone but himself. "Well, Elias ain't rotten. He's a real nice person. Just be up front with me, though, you know? If you're gay, that's fine. You don't need to hit on me like that. Or if you need something, just ask. You don't have to do all that other bullshit. I'll do what I can to help you."

"Like hiding intentions is worse than the actual thing?" I posed to him.

"Yeah." He slapped the back of his hand against his palm. "Like earlier today, I was afraid to ask you about the bus card 'cause I didn't know what you'd ask in return. Most guys I know would've held that above my head." Immediately when we woke up, Clyde came up to me and said he needed to holler at me. When we walked out the shelter door, he asked if I had an extra bus card. I could tell it was tough for him. He twisted his body and winced when he asked.

Clyde's chest moved up and down rapidly, like our conversation stressed him out. He changed the subject. "Tell me more about where you're from. You're from the country, right?" Clyde's directness threw me. I pushed myself off the wall, kicking my backpack, and moved closer to him. The women behind us in line listened in on our conversation.

"Uh, yeah, Wisconsin." Clyde yearned to know more about my rural background. It made me realize only a few college classmates ever did.

"You ever drive a tractor?" he asked.

I laughed. "Yeah, plenty."

"Big ones?" He scrunched up his face.

"Uh huh." I nodded. "Big-ass ones with those huge tires."

"Damn." He jerked his head, one of the few movements he made during the conversation. "You ever get scared ridin' them? I think it'd be cool driving a truck—like those huge rigs, but I don't know how. That'd take a lot of skill and responsibility." The women behind us nodded their heads.

"Yeah, sometimes I get freaked out. Like if I'm ridin' up a hill." I reclined backward. "I get nervous about tipping over." I grabbed Clyde's arm tightly. "I grip the steering wheel and seat like this!" He stared into my eyes, captivated. "Or I've hauled full wagons down the road. That's made me nervous. There's so much weight and money behind me—probably like if you drove a truck." I hit his arm. "I just pray I get to the next place safely!" I laughed. The women's eyes widened as they covered their mouths with their hands.

"See, I don't have those skills like you," Clyde muttered. He dipped his head and adjusted his bandana.

"It's just second nature, that's all. Just like you in the city—you know way more than me."

He shrugged. "The city must be a lot different for you," he said.

"What'd you think?"

"Umm. It's not bad. There's a lot going on. I was always mesmerized by all the lights and buildings, you know? It's the suburbs that I probably can't do," I admitted.

He nodded his heavy head. The door opened and the rustled noises grew louder and chatter increased. The line began moving step by step. Clyde and I waited patiently, yet anxiously hoping what we needed would still be there.

Clyde turned his body to me. "What're you lookin' for, Rick?"

"I could use a coat since it's getting cold."

"Yeah, that's important. I got one at my sister's." He mimed bundling a coat.

"What about you?" I asked.

"A belt," he replied. "I think I've been losin' more weight from walking' around, scrappin' all day." He stuck his thumb in the front of his jeans and stretched it forward. Even though we needed different things, we shopped together.

We walked inside and took in a whiff of used clothes. It smelled like an old attic but with a slight scent of body odor. The mustard-yellow walls made the space look tighter than reality. "There's a coatrack over there." Clyde pointed. I hurried over to beat anyone else near me. Clyde tailed at his own pace.

I shuffled through the coats, one after the other, and then came across a thick gray coat.

"That one's nice," Clyde said. I threw it around my shoulder and inserted my arms. "Fits too," Clyde added.

I looked at myself in the large mirror and rotated my body like a model. "Hmm. Yeah, I think you're right. I'm gonna keep this."

"That'll keep you warm as this weather keeps droppin'."

We continued walking around, keeping our eye out for belts. I was surprised not to see any of my other friends initially, but remembered the free store was only open for such a brief time. They had stuff going on. Not to be too picky, but the quality of the clothing was extremely poor. Of the shirts I rummaged through, several had holes. Almost all had stains. I could find better ones for a quarter at a thrift store. While the gesture of free clothing and accessories was appreciated—and many took advantage of it—it felt degrading to be offered the clothing in its shape. My stomach knotted with unease. Numerous items I saw should've ended up in the trash. I thought back to my conversation with Reid, and how it was assumed a homeless individual would eat our pizza because it was food. Whoever donated the free store clothing probably used the same assumption—that the homeless will wear anything because they're homeless. It reinforced the homeless stigma within society.

I spotted a faded brown belt. "What about this?" I handed it to Clyde. He examined it for one second, and then shoved it through the loops on his jeans. He put it through the metal buckle and tugged.

Snap! The belt broke into two. I snorted, but Clyde looked un-amused. He flashed me a death stare.

He reached for a purple and orange, cotton-woven strap with no buckle. He repeated the looping process and tied a knot in front. It satisfied the basic need. Then he asked me a question that seemed out of the blue. "Rick, you notice how at Rawls, all the volunteers get to smoke, but we don't?"

I tilted my head. "What'd you mean?"

"They can't legally do that."

I pinched my eyebrows together. "How so?"

Clyde waved his hand. "There's a contract there, and they're violating the terms. They have to allow everyone the same opportunity."

"How do you know that?" I probed.

"I studied law in prison."

"What?" My body collapsed halfway to the ground. The revelation shocked me.

"Guys will study law all the time," he explained. "They try to get something changed about their case. When I realized there was nothing I could do on mine, I turned to civil law. I know all about the courts and almost every state's constitution."

"Really?" My interest drew me so close that I stepped into Clyde's personal space. He didn't flinch.

"A lot of times, these attorneys do a sloppy job. Sometimes the guys who are locked up for like a hundred years or life will be real sharp on everything and help out other guys. It's sort of their way to have a purpose and get back at people."

"Shoot! You should be my lawyer if I ever need one," I said. "You got all this knowledge and you want to be a truck driver?"

"I can't. I'm a felon."

My shoulders deflated at those words.

Clyde was the most interesting man I had ever met. Our lives had been so different, but we got along. He was smart and worked hard. I wondered where he'd be if he grew up in a different environment.

The CEO of a Fortune 500 company? A high-profile lawyer? An engineer designing Chicago's next big skyscraper? His potential was endless, but his environment, and the decisions he made within it, limited him. I knew he wasn't the only one whose story turned out that way.

CHAPTER EIGHTEEN

A SOBER SUNDAY

"Time to get up!" Andre bellowed. The daily 5:45 wakeup call didn't bother me, but getting up an hour earlier on Sunday was brutal. No snooze button existed. I rubbed my eyes and lifted my body from the mat. The grogginess never wore off till breakfast, but packing up my belongings became an automatic routine.

A few guys remained curled up on their mat, hoping to catch a few more minutes of rest. Andre made the rounds, hovering over each person for added encouragement.

A man slowly crept to Andre.

"I think my brother's dead," he said.

"You think your brother's dead?" Andre repeated. The man silently nodded. If he slumped any further, he'd fall to the floor. He stared at Andre for answers.

They were identical twins in every sense. The pair of middle-aged men never left each other's side. They stood on the stairs together; they ate dinner together; they waited in the shower line together; they slept with their mats side by side. Even their receded hairlines were the same.

Andre escorted the man back to a mat, where a man in jeans was still curled up on his side. He never bothered taking off his scuffed Adidas pro-models before bed.

A quiet, eerie vibe lingered. By this point, the remaining men inside the shelter took notice. They stood, frozen in place, watching Andre and the brother. I did the same. The twins slept near me during the night—only a row of mats separated us.

Andre squatted beside the mat and placed his fingers on the man's neck. Crushed hope covered his face. He rested his arm on his knee and paused.

"Is he?" the brother asked.

Andre stood up and bowed his head. The man's already-puffed face grew more exaggerated. He stared through Andre with limped arms at his side. His world literally changed overnight. I believe his mind worked so hard to comprehend his loss that he forgot to cry.

"Do you want to call anyone?" Andre asked, but he didn't respond. Andre repeated, "Do you want to call anyone? Your daughter, maybe?"

The man shook his head.

"You don't have anyone you want to call?"

"No," he mumbled.

I never expected to experience anything like this when I chose to live homeless. It didn't cross my mind that I'd see a dead body. I continued staring at the corpse. It didn't make sense to me. The night before, an energy filled that same body. I saw it. And now it was gone. It made me believe souls existed. Spirituality was something that had always been on my mind, but I never made the effort to dig deeper, to reflect on it more. As a twenty-two-year-old, it wasn't at the top of my priority list. That morning forced it upon me. My grogginess disappeared; my mind raced.

From the corner of my eye, I noticed Jarris joined me. His studded earrings didn't shine. The room was still dark and the sun hadn't peaked from the horizon.

"I overheard he mixed alcohol and crack," Jarris muttered, gazing at the body.

"Damn. For real?" I hung my head. Of course it had to be that and not something natural to debunk the stereotype that homeless individuals abused drugs.

"That's what some guys were sayin'." I could only shake my head. Jarris appeared different. He didn't have the relentless enthusiasm I grew accustomed to. He looked rocked. He had no expression on his face.

"Come on"—Jarris turned and nudged me—"let's get outta here." He couldn't look at the body any longer.

We trudged toward the exit. The brother followed Andre into his office. We heard loud sobs and sniffs. He finally broke down. Jarris and I flashed worried looks at each other.

We climbed up the steps. Paramedics marched past us as we walked through the doorway.

Neither of us said a word as we turned onto Jackson for our mile-long hike to the blue line. The air felt colder than most mornings. The vacant buildings and inactive streets never bothered me till now. Loneliness surrounded us. The death forced us to reflect on our own mortality, something that never crossed our minds as the youngest men in the shelter, which concerned the older guys. We had so much life ahead, we assumed.

"Hey!" Jarris shoved me. My head shot up. I lost focus of the sidewalk cracks. "Look!" He pointed ahead. A long, navy-blue van violently veered from one sidewalk to another. "She's drunk!" Jarris shouted.

"Shit!" My stomach dropped. I stared at it, frozen.

"Over here." Jarris grabbed my arm and pulled me to the bus shelter ten feet back. "She's gotta see us—she wouldn't hit us, right?" He stared at my face for an answer. I didn't have one for him.

The van continued swerving at an uncontrollable speed.

She drove closer. Jarris put his arm on my shoulder.

And closer.

She headed right at us.

We bit our lips, wincing.

Screeeeech! The van missed the shelter.

"The fuck!" I yelled. I flipped my angry finger at the van, already farther down the street.

We turned to each other and exhaled.

I couldn't feel my body. It was weightless. My movements appeared from afar, like I floated above my body. It was a wooziness combined with adrenaline. I gasped for air. Jarris and I struggled to say anything to each other. What were we supposed to say? Our eyes said enough. They were locked on each other. We escaped a tragedy, our possible death. We thought we escaped death when we walked out the shelter door, but now it became even more real on the streets of Chicago.

CHAPTER NINETEEN

ARMANDO'S BACK

"Hey!" Farouk jumped into the van, squeezing me against the window. It was colder outside. I was glad I found the coat in the free store. Once seated, we began our journey to Rawls. "I'm going to Truman College," Farouk said.

"Yeah? That's great." Attending college as a homeless individual had to be more challenging than going as an average joe. The paperwork would be a nightmare. The logistics of where to keep books and school materials would be a headache. Farouk had an uphill battle in store. "What're you gonna study?" I asked.

"Journalism," he responded.

"What're you interested in covering?"

"Politics and sports," he replied. "Test me. Ask me any questions about the Bulls."

"Hmm. Okay." I stroked my beard. "How many MVPs does Michael Jordan have?"

"Five!" Farouk answered.

"That's true." I lifted my finger to my lip. "How many MVPs

does Scottie Pippen have?"

"He doesn't have any." Farouk laughed with closed eyes. "You're trying to trick me."

I chuckled. "I'm just testing you, Farouk. That's what you wanted."

"I'm really excited to go to school. I'm taking an exam at one thirty tomorrow. Will you pray for me?" Farouk asked.

"Yeah. I will." College alone could be tough. With Farouk living homeless, it would be tougher. He could use all the help he could get.

Phil turned up the radio. "You Are Everything" by The Stylistics came on. Farouk closed his eyes and swayed back and forth. During my time staying at Rawls, my music horizon had expanded. The music we listened to provided me a snapshot into my friends' young lives. Farouk's musical palette had probably changed since he arrived from Africa too. Certain male artists played in rotation: Al Green, Stevie Wonder, Marvin Gaye, The Bee Gees, The Meters, Parliament, Michael Jackson, and The Stylistics. Music from the '70s and '80s provided the soundtrack around me.

The song ended and Farouk turned to me and confessed, "I stopped smoking weed and drinking. Are you proud of my maturity?"

"I am. Way to go." We bumped fists. Farouk squinted at my forehead and then pointed to my eyes. "You hair is in your eyes." I shrugged. "If my hair did that, I'd cut it right away. You look like a young Santa Claus with your beard."

"So you better be good then!"

"Oh, yeah," he said, chuckling.

We continued riding down Ashland Avenue.

"I can name a bunch of dead celebrities too," Farouk boasted to me.

"All right. Name some," I replied.

"Marilyn Monroe." He stuck out his index finger. I nodded my head, urging him to continue. "Michael Jackson." He counted two on his hand. "Martin Luther King Jr. Courtney Love. Michael Jackson."

I laughed. "You said Michael Jackson twice." And I was pretty sure Courtney Love was still alive.

"Oh!" He palmed his forehead. I helped him remember more.

"What about Malcolm X?" I suggested.

"Yeah! He's one."

"Walter Payton?" I said. Farouk nodded. "John Lennon," I continued.

"You're good," Farouk remarked.

Suddenly, I felt a familiar poke on the back of my neck. I sprang forward and looked behind me. Armando smiled, his switchblade in hand. My survival instincts kicked in immediately. My heart raced and my mind focused.

"Stop it, man!" I snapped. I tried to balance on the tightrope of passiveness, but something like this was uncalled for. "This is the second time you've done that. I told you not to." He snickered and didn't move. Pete and Julius watched from the corners of their eyes with scowled faces. I knew they had my back.

"I was just joking," Armando said. "I like you. You're laidback.

Remember when we drank together? That was fun, man." I hadn't seen Armando in a while. His personality remained the same. He blew it off like it wasn't a big deal. He liked to note that we came from different backgrounds and, in mine, you didn't pull a switchblade on someone as a joke. And when someone told you to stop, you stopped doing whatever the person didn't like.

He forced a conversational transition by pulling a bottle of cologne from his bag.

"Check out this cologne." He sprayed himself and showed me the bottle. "You want any?" He held it out like an olive branch, a lame apology for pulling a knife on me a second time.

"It smells nice," I said, "but I'll pass because I'm going to a shelter full of guys." I wasn't willing to accept it.

"Yeah, that's right!" Reggie turned around from the passenger seat, aggressively nodding. "Rick is right."

"Well, sometimes you got to present yourself good. You know? Just because you're homeless doesn't mean you have to look or smell homeless," Armando said.

Everyone bobbed their heads. "I feel you," Reggie said.

Armando groomed himself, brushing his hair. "Do your feet ever hurt from walking around so much?"

I had cooled off a bit. I thought I made my point clear to him. "Uh, sometimes I get blisters and stuff," I replied.

"I got shot in my leg once by a .38 Special. They put a steel rod in there so now when it gets cold out, my leg hurts."

"Is that why I see you limpin' around?" I asked brashly.

"Yeah," Armando replied. "So how long are you gonna grow your beard?"

"I don't know." I shrugged. "I don't intend to cut it anytime soon."

"You're a four-eyed Chuck Norris." Armando smiled. He leaned his elbows onto the back of my bench and switched to a softer tone. "So have you talked to your mom recently?"

"I emailed her again, but no response," I said.

"Maybe you should take the next step—maybe call her. You want to make sure you're still on her mind. You know what they say, 'Out of sight, out of mind.' Put your pride behind you."

"Yeah, that's true." I tilted my head to one side. "Oh, hey!" I said. "Do you have that ten dollars I lent you awhile back?"

He squirmed, tilting his head. "I've been getting some jobs lately, and I'll eventually pay you back—even if it's little by little," he declared. "I bought a cake for one of my daughters and my son for their birthdays. I didn't have much left over after."

I narrowed my eyes. I stayed disciplined with my budget. Ten dollars got me a lot. I could do my laundry four times, buy nine coffees from McDonald's or twenty bars of soap. I lent money to other guys, and they each paid me back. My view of Armando soured quickly, even after he made nice by asking about my mother.

Pete pointed out the window. "Man, look how dark it gets on this street. Only a couple blocks earlier, it was bright as day. That's the most obvious sign of gentrification I've seen," he said. "I remember going to concerts at Chicago Stadium. The neighborhoods didn't look pristine like that—probably all changed when they built the United Center."

We stopped at an intersection. A man in a wheelchair approached the van. Before he could speak, Phil rolled down the window and stuck his hand out.

"Whatchya got for me today?" Phil beckoned. All the guys in the van laughed. The man looked down, laughing. His shoulders vibrated up and down.

He pointed at Phil. "You beat me to it. I'm supposed to ask *you* that!"

The light turned green.

"Well, we gotta run," Phil said. "Go six blocks east—the lights are brighter there." The man showed a toothless grin.

Phil twisted his body around to us. "I don't know what that guy's doin'—this area ain't no good. Why do you guys think I give out them passes so quick when we get to Rawls? I don't want to be over here."

"Tell me about it." Julius sprung his arm forward. "In all those years in the army, going to all those countries, it wasn't till I got back to the west side that I got shot." He was half-serious, half-joking. The rest of us north-siders gulped and nodded with uneasiness.

Journal Entry — October 15, 2011

I woke up at 3:45 a.m. and couldn't fall back asleep. One guy coughed the whole night, spitting in a Dixie cup next to his mat. It reminded me to take care of my immune system, especially now that the weather is colder. I guess, though, it's not the weather that concerns me, it's my stress. It's become a massive struggle. Each day feels like an eternity. I don't feel free. I feel constrained. The process of living in a shelter drags me through each day like how a toddler recklessly cares for his toys.

I see more new faces at Rawls every night. It feels like everyone's tensions are higher and patience is growing scarcer. Staying positive is challenging. I've finally realized what my goal is this month. It's to stay warm and keep my sanity.

CHAPTER TWENTY

IT'S INTERESTING, BEING HOMELESS

"The preacher's cheatin'!" Reggie yelled.

Whack! Reggie swatted the chessboard onto the ground. Everyone in the garage looked over to him. I exhaled a cloud of smoke from the corner of my mouth as I leaned against the wall.

"He says he's a godly man, but he cheats!" Reggie paced back and forth. The preacher remained sitting at the table, waiting for Reggie's outburst to end.

The preacher was a black man with dreadlocks and a white goatee, whose thick Bible never left his hand. Most guys I knew didn't like him. He was pretentious. He lectured others about God, evangelizing his own interpreted theology as gospel itself. When others felt inspired to share their spirituality, the preacher shot them down and arrogantly explained why they were wrong. His calm, pompous attitude turned others off.

I wasn't particularly fond of him either, but I didn't think he cheated. I was sure that he beat Reggie fair and square. Reggie was just sour and knowing that made his overly dramatic performance more hysterical. If he couldn't win at chess, at least he could fulfill his need for attention.

"Can't wait till your judgment day, preacher!" Reggie waved around his finger. "God's finna say, 'You's a spiritual man, yes, but what about that time you cheated 'cause you's afraid to cry?'" Reggie stomped up the steps and pouted. "Those are sins!" He marched past me through the dayroom doorway. Everyone in the garage laughed in amusement. We got a free show.

Elias and Julius sat together at a table. I meandered over, pulling up an old dining-room chair. "What're you guys talkin' about?" I asked.

"Oh, hey, Rick!" Elias beamed. Julius extended his arm for a handshake. His cheeks glowed. "I was just saying how I interviewed for a job and they called back, but I was in the middle of another interview, so I couldn't answer it. They didn't even leave a voicemail." Elias grunted and shook his head. "It's hard enough, you know?"

"Sorry to hear that," I said, patting his shoulder. "That sucks. Do you have their phone number? Maybe you can follow up."

"Somewhere in here." He bent over searching through numerous loose sheets of paper in his bag.

"Well, make sure you try to find it," I implored. "How's everything else? Still not liking the situation upstairs?" I asked, gesturing to the apartment above me.

Elias sat back in his seat, contorting his face. "Eh. Hopefully I don't stay much longer." He crossed his fingers. "I think I might get into the YMCA soon."

"Nice, man! That's awesome," I said. Julius patted him on the back.

"Yeah, this whole thing's interesting—being homeless." Elias sighed with a humble smile. "I learned more than I bargained for. It's something I didn't really understand fully until I was on the inside. I remember the first shelter I stayed at was Sacred Life. I didn't know any better. I just went wherever DHS told me."

"Sacred Life?" Julius blurted. Elias raised his eyebrows and pursed his lips.

"I've only heard folktales about it. What was it like for you?" I implored.

"I stayed there four nights. Don't go there!" he warned us. "You have to get up at five o'clock every morning. If you want breakfast, which is only watery oatmeal and a stale pastry, you have to attend a religious service. For lunch, which is only soup and a sandwich, you have to attend another religious service. And for dinner, which is also soup and a sandwich—you guessed it—another religious service. The food is awful." He stuck his tongue out.

"Jeez," I uttered. It sounded cult-ish to me. His descriptions of meals made me think of a Charles Dickens book, where poor characters were fed gruel. Authorities took advantage of the people and viewed them as numbers.

Elias continued, "Oh, and to go to bed, you have to go to another religious service. And if that's not enough for you, they have Bible studies during the day. I'm religious"—he pressed his chest—"but they're extreme!"

"I've heard others say that too," Julius said, nodding in agreement.

"If you need any resources for jobs or medical help, you can only use them—nowhere else. It's really disappointing because I've found a lot of other helpful services in the city. Why should you be limited?" Elias's red face fumed. "It's a place that just keeps people homeless." He pointed to his head. "They brainwash the homeless there—and they can because it's their way or the highway. If you don't like it—go!"

"People make careers of it, you know?" Julius professed to Elias. "It happens. I don't know why someone would, but they do, and they master their profession." As unfortunate as it was, Julius was right. I saw it at both Rawls and Inspired Horizons. However, I didn't believe it was just a simple decision that an individual made one day: "Yeah, this is what I'm going to do with my life." It was more like a decision made after years of struggle, most of which I believed started with the tragedy of being born into the wrong situation. The idea of the American Dream convinced the rest of society that if these individuals tried harder, they, too, could overcome their obstacles. The American Dream allowed society not to take responsibilities of its neighbors' well-being.

But without places like Rawls and Inspired Horizons taking in "Hall-of-Famers," as others referred to them, the shelter and organization couldn't help others who still had hope. They needed the numbers Hall-of-Famers supplied in order to maintain funding to ensure resources were available. I met men from all over the state, country, and world because, somehow, they learned that Chicago had resources to help people improve their lives as well as their families' lives.

I said, "Pete told me he only lasted thirty minutes there."

A smile broke on Elias's face. "Oh, goodness! He would not do well there." He shook his head, grinning.

"He said he told the case manager he was Catholic, and they got into a loud argument. Said he stomped down the hallway cussin' the place out," I elaborated. "Classic."

"That man's headstrong," Julius said. "Nothin' wrong with that— gotta put your foot down when something's not right." I figured part of Julius's philosophy stemmed from his military background, which Pete shared.

"How does it compare to Rawls?" I asked Elias.

"Well, everything is cleaner."

"That's not a high bar," I joked.

"No. It's not!" Elias smiled. "It's almost *too* clean." He squinted.

"What?" *How can a homeless shelter be too clean?*

"It's too sterile," Elias said, pushing his long hair behind his ear. "There's no character. Five hundred men and five hundred women stay there—"

"Holy shit!" I gasped. Julius raised his eyebrows and echoed my exclamation.

"Yeah. You're just a number there. You're herded around like cattle. It's a homeless factory." Images from Charles Dickens books flashed through my head again. I pictured workhouses and factories during the Industrial Revolution.

"That's a shame," Julius muttered. He scratched his cheek.

"I've heard good things about this place called Emergence," Elias said. "A lot of the guys from Rawls go there during the day. I hear it's in an even worse neighborhood than Rawls, a mile northwest, but the building and inside is top-notch bar none. You have to apply and get accepted into it, though. The food is fantastic. They don't feed you like you're in a shelter."

"Pete told me Bright Oasis is also good one," I said. "I guess they're turning that one into a veteran-only shelter, though. He said it was the best shelter in Chicago. Guys have to help with tasks like cleaning and stuff, but it's solid."

"I tried to get into this one up in Evanston but had interviews and missed my opportunity. It at least would've been interesting to see what it's like," Elias said. He reached into his disorganized bag, feeling around for a few seconds, and pulled out off-brand granola bars. "You guys want one?"

"Sure," Julius answered. Elias handed us both a green package. The bars were oats and honey-flavored. I opened mine right away and bit into one bar. Crumbs fell everywhere. I looked down and picked up the ones that landed in my lap and put them in my mouth.

Julius leaned toward Elias's feet and picked up a newspaper that fell out of Elias's bag. He set it on the table and pointed to a picture on the front page and said, "I think he's going to be our next president."

Elias lurched forward. I stood up and bent closer. Tinier crumbs in my lap fell to the ground. Julius's large thumb pressed on a photo of Texas Republican Governor Rick Perry.

"Don't get me wrong. Obama is inspirational. But I think Perry will win. I like some of his ideas." My head tilted automatically. I had only met one other black Republican in my short life.

Julius noticed my inquisitive look. "Let me tell you—black people used to vote Republican. Abe Lincoln freed them, and he was Republican. A lot of Democrats were from the South, and they were racist. Once FDR came in, and then Kennedy in the 1960s, they started voting Democrat," he explained, slapping the back of his hand into his palm. Elias and I focused directly on his passionate eyes. "America started screwing up when all these 'free-thinking' movements happened. Back then, a black father could discipline his kids. I'm not talking about abuse, but a slap on the *behind*. Sons respected their mother because she disciplined them too." He pounded the table with his fist. It wobbled off balance, distracting Julius for a brief second.

Someone reclined in a lawn chair by the wall, charging his phone, and looked in our direction. He looked back down and continued texting.

Julius regained control again. "But then the government started giving more money to single-mother families, and so the women drove the men out of the house. They didn't need the income from men anymore." He threw his palms up. "It's ridiculous! The government punished families for being together and rewarded living single instead. Black people haven't voted differently in thirty years, and I don't think they know why."

I rubbed my bearded chin, thinking about what Julius said. He sounded old school, like he belonged to an older generation. It sounded personal too—perhaps his family split up during that time and he resented it. Or maybe a woman left him. I hoped he hadn't physically abused anyone. From every interaction with him, that seemed impossible. He was one of the most charming and delightful men I'd met. I hesitated to ask. Instead, Elias slid in his opinion about the government.

"That's when the government ballooned too," Elias added. "Social Security stuck around after its intended purpose and, if you ask me, it's one big Ponzi scheme." Julius nodded forcefully.

The man in the lawn chair glanced over again, distracted by the commotion. It was hard not to be distracted when these guys got passionate about certain topics.

Julius said, "You look around and a lot of people take advantage of the system. If the government needs to be involved, they need to reward hard work rather than just handing out assistance to everyone." He pounded his fist again. "That being said, make sure people with disabilities and stuff get what they need."

I crossed my arms and leaned back in my chair. Listening to their political opinions fascinated me. America always seemed divided into two belief systems, but in reality, every voter was different. Every Republican and every Democrat didn't always support *every* issue of their party—and they could weigh one issue more than another. It reminded me of homelessness. In reality, every homeless person was different. Their resources differed, and the cause of their situation varied. The stereotype of the homeless was not absolute.

Journal Entry — October 17, 2011

I've been in contact with my parents through email. I shoot my mom an email each time I'm at the library typing my journal, which is three to four times a week. It's kind of strange I'm in contact with my parents more while homeless than in college. Should I have been in touch more in school?

The emails are pretty uneventful. They're usually just to check in and let them know I'm fine. They're worried about me, which I completely understand. Most of the emails consist of what my parents are up to, my brother playing sports and adjusting to high school, my little sister's involvement in extracurricular school activities, and my older sister and her boyfriend and what they're up to. She's kept me updated on the progress of harvest season on the farm. I've told them some stories about people I've met and things I've learned—the PG version, of course, so they don't freak out.

I appreciate my mom being so concerned. I know I tell people in the shelter, "My mom and I don't really get along," but that's an exaggerated aspect of our true relationship. I've never met a more selfless and loving individual. In our emails, she even looks at the weather forecasts and hopes I'm prepared and able to stay warm. She's the sweetest.

She dedicated her life to raising my siblings

and me, but now that we've grown older and more independent, I think she's struggling with her purpose. I understand the difficulty and how she might feel. She told me she's been looking for part-time jobs and was offered a position making toffee for a candy shop. It's not something she dreamed of doing, but I think she might find some satisfaction from it.

The emails have gotten more intense lately. My aunt's cancer came back, and she's going to have to endure chemotherapy for three months. She's having a tough time, knowing the last three months of chemo were unsuccessful. I've kept her in my thoughts.

My mom says my little sister asks about me more and more. She said she misses me a lot. One of my former teachers and her husband died in a motor-cycle accident, and my sister is having a tough time with it. She wishes I were back and doesn't understand why we haven't been in contact. I feel really bad about it. I'll eventually let her know what's going on when I feel the time is right. I don't want to be an additional worry for her. She's such a tremendous individual. I admire her. She's so compassionate for others. I wish I were as inspiring and strong as her.

CHAPTER TWENTY-ONE

FRIENDSHIP

Alone at the table, I shivered and blew on my hands to keep warm. Wet clothes covered my body because Rawls didn't have any towels again. I longed for a hot shower all day; it gave me something to look forward to in the rain and cold. I felt blue, down in the dumps. The Sudoku puzzle distracted me from the fact that volunteers carelessly left the door open when they stepped outside to smoke. The chilly drafts made the shelter colder than it needed to be.

"Slick Rick. Smoothest white guy here!" Andre looked me up and down. "You all right?"

I overcompensated to hide my depression and shouted, "Yeah! For sure!" He smiled, reassuring me he'd ignore my awkward delivery. I gave him a slight smile back to show I appreciated it. "Where've you been the last few days?" I asked.

"I needed a break—get outta here for a bit," he said.

"I hear ya." I dipped my head. I understood how he felt. Everyone did. Guys escaped the shelter to keep their sanity. Some stayed in motels; some stayed in the park; some stayed on the L; some stayed with friends or family. The number of options varied from person to person; every situation was different. Hardly anyone stayed in the shelter every single night—that was crazy. Why would someone do that to himself? But that's exactly what I did.

When I first entered the shelter program, I wondered if my presence would take away resources from others. A month and half later—though it seemed like a *year* and a half—I sneered at the younger, naïve version of myself. The opposite happened. My presence helped *ensure* that resources remained for others. Phil even used me as an example. "If y'all want the van to continue, be like Slick Rick here. He shows up every single day." Each day, I signed my name a total of three times: before breakfast inside the Inspired Horizons dayroom; entering Rawls at the bottom of the stairs; and before dinner at the kitchen window. Inspired Horizons and Rawls used those signatures to inform the government and donors how many individuals they helped, providing reason for continued funding. What they did with that funding, though, was often a conversation topic among guys. People questioned where the money went, especially on nights with no soap, towels, or bedsheets.

After learning that, occupying a mat every night didn't bother me. The men who stayed at Rawls weren't the types to request pity from society, either. They were tough dudes—independent survivors. Many were professionals, and they knew what to do. Though homelessness was unfortunate, there were worse things. These men knew that and it guided their perspective on life. When I felt down, I tried to keep them in mind. Thinking of others while experiencing my own problems was difficult. It's an exercise I—and probably most people—needed to get better at.

"I'm as hungry as a grizzly bear," Reggie announced, standing in front of Farouk and me. "Rick, if you don't want your food tonight, I'll take it."

I laughed. "All right. What're we havin'?"

"Hmmm." Reggie leaned forward and shouted to the front of the line, "Hey! What's the chef got today?"

A thin man turned around and answered, "Meatballs and cheese in a tortilla."

"Oh! Them 'dillas, huh?" He snapped his fingers. Reggie rotated his body back to me and, at an obnoxious volume, relayed, "Meatball quesadillas."

"I know, Reggie. I know." I laughed. "I could hear him. I'm standing a foot away from you. And it's the best meal at Rawls. I'm gonna eat everything tonight."

"What!" Reggie pouted. "Come on, Rick!"

"Sorry, man. I'm not passing this up." The quesadillas looked simple, but they packed a punch. It was the only meal I ever recall asking others if they were going to eat all of theirs.

"Humph." Reggie faced forward to protest my decision.

I pivoted to Farouk. "How's school going?" I asked.

"I only took the test so far. School starts in November."

"Oh, okay. It'll be here before you know it."

He shifted his body weight and pointed his finger in the air, like a scientist about to state a fact. "My test says I have a seventh grade reading level." He elaborated, "And I have a good pre-algebra score." His reading level seemed low to me, but I had the education level of a college graduate. I didn't know the quality of education he received in Nigeria. Farouk appeared proud. Perhaps his marks were impressive compared to others he knew. "I'm growing and maturing!" He smiled widely.

"But didn't you tell me yesterday you got arrested for panhandling?" I played devil's advocate.

"That's irrelevant." He flipped his hand with a wider smile.

"All right, fair enough." The shelter warmed up a little, but it was still cold. Maybe waiting in line with others helped. I looked at the basketball hoop, hovering above the line ten feet in front of us. "So are you excited for the Bulls this season?" I asked Farouk.

He crossed his arms and cocked his head. "They're in a lockout right now," he replied like a know-it-all.

"Well, I know that. But when they come back, I mean."

"Yeah, they'll be good," he stated bluntly. "They have Derrick Rose."

"Are you good at basketball, Farouk?" Strangely, from the corner of my eye, I noticed more and more guys in line listening to our conversation. I usually didn't like attention in the shelter, but talking with Farouk relaxed me. I never felt on edge around him.

"The main sport in Nigeria is soccer, but I wasn't good at that, so I played basketball. I didn't start playing till I was fifteen. But even though I started so late, I'm still really good. I can jump really high."

"How high?" I asked.

Farouk stretched his arms as wide as he could.

"No way." I laughed until a cough emerged from the back of my throat. I bent over wheezing as he continued to exaggerate his skill. Others in line laughed too. Some of the their laughing coughs sounded worse than mine. "That's like five feet!"

"Yes, I can," he insisted with a finger pointed in the air again. He wore a serious face.

"You sure?" I tilted my head. He nodded defiantly. I squatted to the ground and positioned my hand a foot above the ground. I looked to Farouk and said, "This is how high I can jump."

He chuckled. "That's not high at all."

The line moved forward. "Well, Farouk, when we get back to Horizons, you should prove you can jump as high as you claim."

"I can show you now." Farouk pointed to the old basketball hoop above us.

His determination surprised me. Most people would've been embarrassed or too shy to perform in front of others, but not Farouk. He didn't care about how it'd make him look. It was part of the childlike enthusiasm I admired about him. Deep down, I was a little jealous of his quality.

He removed his oversized coat and tossed it on the floor. He rubbed his hands together. The room grew quiet. I looked around and couldn't believe how many guys eagerly watched. No one made a sound. The stereo wasn't on, either. It was silent at Rawls, like the middle of the night. Focused stares stretched the faces of all the tired men. Like me, they also appreciated Farouk's energy.

"Hey, look over here"—Farouk pointed at me—"I'm going to prove it to you."

I raised my eyebrows. "You sure you don't need to stretch first?"

Farouk laughed, shaking his head. He started fifteen feet away. He ran closer.

And launched himself, extending his arms to touch the rim. It felt like I watched in slow motion.

His hands barely grazed the grungy, discolored net. He fell epically short of his claim. The room erupted loudly. Guys cried from laughter. A shit-eating grin covered Farouk's face. I shook my head and smiled. I was proud of him for even trying. My heart beamed with happiness.

———

"Listen up, y'all," Andre demanded. He walked to the middle of the room where he broadcasted most of his announcements. "We're not gonna have any bedsheets tonight, but I promise we'll have them tomorrow." Jeers and groans filled the room. Many rolled their eyes.

"I'll believe that when I see it," one guy said condescendingly to his neighbor.

"Also," Andre continued, "I know it's been cold, but the heat will be on soon."

"Don't let volunteers go outside and smoke," someone belted. "That's the real issue!"

"Yeah! They're the only ones allowed to smoke, and they make it cold for the rest of us," another guy shouted.

Andre pushed both hands down simultaneously, indicating for us to calm down. "I know it's cold right now," Andre acknowledged. "But the heat will be on soon. I swear!" He treaded lightly, like a politician in a town hall meeting. He faced a restless audience tired from excuses and demanded action.

I remained on my chair, motionless. The day continued to worsen for me. I removed my glasses and rubbed my eyes and hot forehead. I looked at Pete as I put them back on.

Suddenly, we started laughing. We reached our threshold of unfortunate events. I experienced the feeling before on road trips with friends. Unpredictable occurrences threw a wrench at our carefully planned ideas or itineraries. The control was out of our hands. The only thing to do was smile and accept it—to try to stay positive.

"All right! Can't wait till tomorrow night," Pete said.

"Let's do this!" I mirrored his enthusiasm. A new guy, sitting in the other chair next to me, remained baffled.

"So does this always happen?" he asked.

Pete and I smiled with amusement.

I patted him on the back. "Welcome to Rawls!"

Journal Entry — October 19, 2011

I had a terrible day. The weather was so crummy, I thought back to the lowest point—the van ride to Rawls. My jeans were wet and my socks were soaked. The fifteen guys made the ride feel especially crowded. I always try to be one of the first people in to get one of the window seats. I thought today it'd especially help me feel less claustrophobic.

The window was fogged up. I couldn't look through it, as if the experience of being home- less has become so intense that it has obstruct- ed my thoughts and reflections. I grew panicky, focusing on all the guys squeezed together. I felt trapped.

I feel like I'm experiencing all these emo- tions, but they're crowded like the van. There's so many inside I don't know what to do with them.

I could only think about how miserable I was. I feel like I've reached my original goal. I've stopped learning new things. A day homeless now feels like eternity.

Before falling asleep, though, I lay on my back. Tears watered my eyes. Again, I thought about my miserable day but realized I was still going to bed happy. In fact, my face hurt from smiling so much. It was a perfect ending to not only a terrible day, but also *any* day. With friends, anything is tolerable—even Inspired Horizons and Rawls. Friendships feed us energy and help us to find positivity, even in grim realities. I feel so humbled to have met friends in the shelter.

Guys don't concern themselves with why someone else is here. Everybody has his own issues, and that's understood. It's more about getting through our individual situations and the shelter system together. No one looks at me differently than they do the next guy. I fit in and I belong. There's so much love. The biggest issue I'm having, though, is when they're *not* around. I don't do well when they're gone.

CHAPTER TWENTY-TWO

REGGIE'S INSIGHT

The train stopped, jolting me forward from my slumber. We arrived at O'Hare. I performed the same routine every Sunday to kill time. I looked around. The car was packed, but there was little movement. Other bundled-up homeless individuals remained curled up. A few people yawned. A few others shifted their bodies. It was a game of Tetris to find the most comfortable sleeping position on the hard seats with several bags of belongings you hoped you could secure.

I rose gingerly from my seat. My back was sore from the hour-long ride from the west side. I rotated my neck till I felt it crack. I stretched my arms above my head. A handful of people with shiny suitcases exited the open train car doors. I followed them out. They were actual travelers.

I contorted my body through the turnstiles and turned left in the direction of Terminal 3. I passed a column that Julius spoke of during our conversation at the library—sure enough, someone slept in his spot. I smiled to myself.

My O'Hare routine had become automatic; my grogginess didn't matter. It was six twenty. I'd travel to Terminal 3, because it had the dimmest lighting of the four passenger terminals, and nap until six fifty. I passed a scheduled flights screen and picked one: flight 3753 from Minneapolis. Estimated arrival: 9:50 a.m. It was my insurance if someone confronted me.

The baggage claim was a ghost town. Without hesitation, I lumbered down to the second-to-last conveyor belt and collapsed onto one of the uncomfortable plastic seats. I lifted my sweatshirt's hood over my head and closed my eyes. I drifted off, dreaming of the people-watching opportunities that awaited me at Terminal 1 in the near future.

"What're you doing?" a voice asked.

"Huh?" I shook a hand off my shoulder. Two heavy white men hovered over me. Their bodies blocked out the fluorescent lighting. One was older with white hair. It looked like he was training the younger security guard how to properly antagonize someone wearing a hoodie, minding their own business.

"Are you traveling?" the older man asked with scornful eyebrows.

I adjusted my posture and shook the cobwebs. "Oh, well, I'm picking up a friend. He's getting in from Minnesota at nine fifty." I squinted. "I think he said his flight number was 3753 or something. I'm taking him to the city on the L."

His shoulders dropped and his eyebrows relaxed. The younger security guard scratched his head.

The white-haired man stuttered, "O-okay." He turned to his partner and tapped him on his chest. The interrogation was over. They turned simultaneously and walked away from me without saying another word. I shook my head and stared at their backs with narrowed eyes.

—————

I dragged myself through the dayroom and plopped my heavy body on the chair next to Pete. He was in the last row of chairs in front of the TV.

"Think I can throw it in his mouth?" Pete showed me a ball of crumpled paper. A childlike grin covered his face. He tilted his head toward Marquis, who sat asleep with his mouth open in an old doctor's waiting room chair. "He woke me up earlier." Pete laughed. "He said I looked too comfortable in my chair."

I bit my lip. "I don't know if that's such a good idea."

Pete paused, looking at the ceiling as he twisted his face. "Hmm. Yeah, you're probably right." He leaned to the ground and stuffed the ball of paper in his tattered backpack.

"Hey, Rick," a voiced called from behind us. Pete and I turned around from our chairs. It was Max, wearing his Oakland Raiders jacket. I hadn't seen him in a while, but he appeared more alert than the last time. His face looked healthier, like the dazed cloud had washed away.

"I've been staying at the Fellowship Circle. I have a case manager working with me," he said.

I smiled shyly. "That's good, man."

"You put weight on too," Pete blurted. I glared at Pete. Mentioning someone's weight had always been taboo.

Max lowered his head. "Yeah, I used to be one-seventy-five. Since I became homeless, I'm up to two hundred." It didn't surprise me. I also put on weight since staying at the shelter, but not twenty-five pounds. Fresh food was rare. Sugar and salt drenched every meal. Many times, I chose not to eat. Max probably skipped less.

"I'm going to Eleanor's Place right now. They have way better resources than Horizons. You should come with me, Rick."

I thought back to the last time we talked, when he offered me pills. "Um, no, I think I'm going to stay here," I replied. "Go ahead. I'm glad you're doing better."

He frowned, nodded, and then walked away.

Pete nudged me. "Did something happen between you two?"

I sighed. "Nothing extreme. One day I was just chillin' in the garage, and he came up to me all fucked up. I don't know what he was on or whatever, but he tried to get me to take the same thing. I don't know. I just wasn't cool with that. I felt like he gave up, and I couldn't trust him."

He frowned. "Oh. Sorry, bud."

"It's all right." I shrugged. "It looks like he's doin' a little better now. I'm glad to see that. I'm still not gonna hang out with him, though." I remembered my morning and grabbed Pete's arm. "Oh! I told you about my Sunday O'Hare routine, right?"

"Yeah. Because the bus doesn't run that early," Pete recalled.

"So today"—I held up two fingers—"two security guards confronted me!"

Pete's face remained unchanged. "They probably followed you. That's happened to me before too."

"Well, what the hell? Why?"

"Have you looked at yourself lately?" Pete asked. "You're wearing raggedy clothes and haven't shaved in like a year. As much as Vinny's comments irritate you, he's right that'd you look different without the beard."

"Well—"

"You look suspicious, Rick." He cut me off. "That's what they're lookin' for: people that don't look like they belong at a place like the airport."

I stared at him begrudgingly.

"Speaking of Vinny earlier," Pete said. "I don't know why him and his dad are still at Rawls. I don't get it." He shook his head. "They're both 'supposedly' disabled vets, but there's absolutely no reason why they should be there. Bright Oasis just received a grant from the government to take in veterans. There's something else there we don't know. Maybe Vinny's getting high or something?"

"Nah. I don't think it's that," I said. "But I think you're right. Something's goin' on we don't know about. I'm concerned, but that's not my business." Pete agreed with a frown.

Suddenly, Reggie burst through the dayroom. He marched toward the front. "Where's Slick Rick at? Where's Slick Rick at?" he shouted, swiveling his head. He spotted me next to Pete and rushed over. "Rick! I saw you walkin' yesterday by Union Station. You's was just lookin' up at all those buildings." He clapped his hands thunderously and began snapping his fingers. "Rick's a good 'ol country boy from Wisconsin, but he likes it here in the big city! He finna stay awhile!"

My heartbeat jumped from the sudden attention from others. A hotness shot to my face and ears. I ignored eye contact with Reggie, smiling helplessly in my chair. It made me feel naïve. *I lived in Chicago for four years, and I still look up at the buildings?*

Reggie found an empty chair and dragged it next to Pete and me. My body temperature returned to normal, and I regained my composure.

"Reggie, where were you last night?" I asked. "I didn't see you at Rawls."

"I was with a girl named Janie," he explained. "I haven't told her I'm homeless yet, but I've been thinking about telling her soon." *How hard was it for a homeless man to spend the night with a woman—or even have the opportunity to pick her up in the first place?* I wondered.

I made eye contact with Pete and then back to Reggie. "Hey, do you guys ever go to bars just to pick up women and have a place to sleep?" Reggie's eyebrows shot into his winter hat. Pete looked at me stupefied, like I was an idiot.

"Of course we do! Are you kidding me?" Pete answered.

I burst into laughter. "Wait. So how do you do that? What's that like?" I inquired.

Reggie spread out his hands, instructing me, "You definitely don't tell 'em you're homeless right away. You need to be up front, but add a little sweetness." He puckered his lips.

"Definitely don't tell her you're homeless right away," Pete echoed Reggie, who shook his head with conviction.

"I told one girl I was homeless the morning after, but she didn't believe me. She said, 'You don't look homeless.' I kept telling her I was, but she didn't believe me. I don't know if she straight up didn't think so or if she was ashamed to be lying next to a homeless man."

"Hmm." I leaned back and pinched my eyebrows together. "In general, how do people respond to you when you tell them you're homeless, Reggie?"

"Well, what people who live paycheck to paycheck don't realize is that they're not far from becoming homeless themselves. You don't think it'll happen to you, but then at some point, you realize you're homeless."

He didn't answer the question, but his response provoked me; I found it profound. I expected him to rise from his chair and enthusiastically describe an encounter, but instead, he explained his homelessness with a subtle grace that hugged both himself and others. It was okay to be homeless. The word *homeless* shouldn't define the individual or their self-worth. The premeditation in his delivery signaled to me that he had contemplated his homelessness before—that in his mind, he combatted the stereotypes affiliated with the issue. Sometimes the ideas and beliefs in our minds affected us more than what physically happened to us. I noticed my own mind lately was clouded with a darkness I wasn't familiar with, and wasn't sure how to handle it.

CHAPTER TWENTY-THREE

CONVICTION OVER ADDICTION

Carpet padding lied on the flooded floor. Water leaked from the tiles next to the shower line. The first couple days, volunteers laid bedsheets over it, but it proved ineffective.

Felipe and I waited in the shower line. Keeping our feet hovered over the flooded ground below us became a tiring exercise.

"Whew!" Felipe said with his signature lisp. "This is a tough workout."

I knew Felipe for over a month. He talked like how I remembered Michelangelo did in the *Teenage Mutant Ninja Turtles* cartoons. He was a highly energetic, short, Nicaraguan man with glasses, dark hair down to his shoulders, and an acne-scarred face. He comprised one-third of "Three Amigos," a nickname dubbed by Andre for Juan, him, and another man, Arturo, a Mexican man with a shaved head. They frequently spoke Spanish to each other, and since few others in the shelter knew the language, they appeared to be friends more than in reality.

We ate dinner together on occasion, but baseball is what bonded us. Felipe loved baseball. All the time, he rattled off stats and stories about players from the '80s and '90s. He brought a portable radio and headphones to the shelter just to listen to playoff games—games that sometimes featured my favorite team, the Milwaukee Brewers. He began cheering for them too.

"I went to the VA today and went to some workshops," Felipe said.

"You're a veteran too? I didn't know that," I replied.

"I'm not, but no one said anything," he admitted. "It was really helpful, though." He pointed to a stack of loose papers and manila folders on the table in front of us. "They gave me résumés and job applications. I plan to study all of it."

"Good for you, man. Certainly can't hurt." He nodded, and then nudged me. Arturo stood up from the table across us and walked away.

"Watch this! I'm gonna prank him."

Felipe jumped off his chair carefully and tiptoed to avoid the water. He reached from the edge of the table, with one leg for better balance, to a bottle of shampoo in front of Arturo's seat. He grabbed it, secured it to his chest, and returned to the shower line, hiding Arturo's shampoo bottle behind him.

"Shhh!" He put his finger on his lips. I gave Felipe a hesitant smile, unsure how Arturo would react since I didn't know him well.

We looked back at the table. Arturo approached with crunched eyebrows.

"*Que carajo! Donde esta!*" he yelled, fumbling around the chairs and bags. Felipe's mouth gaped open, and his mischievous eyes grew larger. "*Que carajo! Donde esta!*" Arturo repeated, throwing his hands in the air. He kicked a metal chair in anger, then scratched his forearm aggressively.

Felipe clutched my shoulder for balance. He turned away, covering his mouth to hide his cackling.

Arturo, finding the search for his shampoo unsuccessful, cracked his knuckles and left the table again to look elsewhere.

Felipe tapped my arm and scurried to the table, returning the bottle of shampoo to its original spot. "Shhh!" He put his finger on his grinning lips once again and crept back to the chair next to me. We didn't wait long before Arturo paced back to his stuff, shaking his head.

"Aw, *estuvo aqui todo el tiempo!*" he shouted to himself when he realized it was right in front of him. Felipe barreled over in laughter but remained attentive of the leaking floor.

Arturo glanced at Felipe with a confused look, not processing he hid it. Arturo slipped right back into a calm demeanor. He folded his shirts and left one on the table for after his shower.

"You're too much, Felipe." I shook my head, smirking. The prank itself was fun, but not knowing the context of their actual friendship made me nervous. As someone who had been consciously walking a tightrope of passiveness, I didn't like that an affiliation with another person's actions was out of my control. If Arturo and Felipe weren't friends, would there have been a fight? Would Arturo tell Andre, and then would I be barred a few nights from Rawls? Neither scenarios were likely, but I was a paranoid person.

I finished brushing my teeth and walked out of the bathroom. Vinny stood by the small set of steps, almost like he waited for me. "I'm getting married on the twentieth next month," he said.

"What?" My eyebrows jumped into my long bangs.

He nodded. "I'm getting married," he repeated with his hands on his hips, like he accomplished a long day's work.

I shook my head in confusion. "When did this come about? How long have you dated her?" Those seemed to be practical questions in my mind.

He raised his chin. "A month ago, my dad and I walked to Navy Pier and that's when I met her."

My neck launched forward. "Dude. That's a month—and you're getting married?"

"She's a nice woman, Rick, and I'm getting old," he explained. "If I want to start a family—and I do—I can't worry about the amount of time I've known her."

I sighed. It still didn't make sense to me. In college, I could go a month without doing laundry. In that same amount of time, someone could meet their soulmate, fall in love, and decide to get married? "All right. I'm happy for you, Vinny. I think that'll be good for you." I reached out my arm and patted his shoulder. "Good luck."

"Thanks, Rick. I think it'll be good too." We shook hands.

I wondered whether his homelessness impacted the decision at all. *Was marrying someone an easy way to attain housing?* Legally, their assets would merge. *Was she homeless too?* The married couples at

Inspired Horizons made it work, with a lot of effort. I spoke to one guy, and he admitted to me that living homeless definitely put a strain on their relationship. And there would be a wedding—Vinny was too old school not to have one. Planning a wedding was stressful enough for most couples; combining that with the logistics of living homeless made my head hurt. I was happy for Vinny, but the logical part of my brain failed to understand it.

I walked back to my chair and leaned against the kitchen wall. Pete sat next to me.

"What's up?" Pete asked. "You look like something's on your mind."

I turned to him. "You're not going to believe this."

"Try me," he insisted.

"Vinny's getting married next month."

Pete flew back in his chair. "You're kidding!"

I waved my open palm. "No, that's what he just told me. He said he's known her for a month."

"Wow. I don't know what surprises me more: the timing of it all or that someone wanted to marry Vinny."

I shrugged. "I don't know, though. For as much as he frustrates me and I try to avoid him, he is a decent guy. He sticks to his principles. You know what you're going to get with him. If a woman is willing to put up with the rest of his personality, he could be a good husband and dad. That's appealing to some women." Pete bobbed his head up and down. "And maybe that's what he needs—someone to take care of him. He takes care of his dad so much that he's probably neglected his own self."

"Yeah, that's true. Good for him," Pete said.

Reggie and Marquis appeared from behind a column. Reggie snapped his fingers like he had just won the lottery. He put his fist in front of me.

"Slick Rick, we're headin' out for the night. Hold down the fort while I'm gone." I bumped his fist with mine.

"All right. Done."

"I'll help him out," Pete assured Reggie.

Reggie waved him off. "Nah. Rick's got it."

Pete and I exchanged smiles. Marquis shook his head with a kind smile and joined a strutting Reggie, already halfway to the door.

"See, now that's love"—Pete pointed to the exit—"he's always like that with Marquis around. You think Vinny's got his fiancée snappin' her fingers like that?"

I laughed. "A love like that—that's what I dream of."

"Be careful. Dreams come true," Pete warned. "My dream is to get out of here."

"Big dreams, baby."

"The biggest!" Pete raised his fist. "I'm makin' it happen too. That's why I wasn't here last night. I didn't get out of the VA till after six thirty. I was tryin' to get some things straightened out. I slept on the blue line last night."

"That's good to hear. How was the blue line?" I asked.

He rolled his eyes. "By three in the morning, the train car was full with other homeless people. Cops walked German shepherds on leashes up and down the aisle."

"Dang. Did they do anything?"

"No. They're there just to intimidate—to scare you into not doing something." He tapped my forearm. "Around six, though, a cleaner woke me up and gave me coffee and two donuts. That made the rough night of rest more tolerable."

In my experience, I had never seen dogs used on the L, at least when I was homeless. I did, however, see a dog used at Union Station. I took a nap. The police used the German shepherd to confront another man lying two benches away from me. I stood up and left. It intimidated me. Using a frightening animal was an easy way to flex authority onto others. It was cheap and unfair but effective. If a cop did that in the middle of the night on the train while I tried to sleep, holding my backpack in my arms, it would have bothered me incredibly. The police were supposed to protect citizens, not bully them. That being said, no one else would think of behaving out of line around me, either. Police canines were a double-edged sword.

I broke eye contact with Pete and squinted past him.

"What?" Pete said, turning around.

"What's Clyde up to?" I wondered aloud. "He's talking to each person along the wall. He doesn't do that."

"I don't know. Looks like he saw you. He's comin' over here." Clyde lumbered toward us. His straight face looked more focused than usual. He carried something on his mind, other than the stress he continually hauled.

"Rick." He tramped closer until he stood in front of me. "Do you have a toothbrush I can use?"

"Oh. Uh, yeah. But it's kinda dirty. I just—"

"That's okay. I don't mind," he said.

"Oh. Um. Hold on." I reached into my backpack and pulled out my marked-up, borderline-moldy Ziploc bag of toiletries. I unzipped it and rummaged around with my hand. "Here you go." I offered the still-wet toothbrush. "Keep it."

"Thanks, Rick. I appreciate it." Clyde took the toothbrush and strode toward the bathroom.

"I've done a lot of crazy things in my life"—Pete confessed—"but I've never used another man's toothbrush. That guy is more fearless than I could ever be." Pete smiled and raised his eyebrows.

"Clyde's somethin' else, man. I've never met anyone like him."

"Chairs up!" Andre announced, startling us out of our conversation.

All the men folded up their chairs. Clanks of metal filled the space between the columns and kitchen wall. Each person carried his chair to a cart by the exit. I handed mine to a volunteer, and he stacked it. Felipe nudged me with a snicker.

"Remember how mad Arturo got earlier?" He had lost his smile from earlier. He sighed. "Man, I used to be like that all the time."

"What'd you mean?" My eyebrows pinched together.

"The withdrawal from heroin. You get angry and agitated for no reason—like misplacing a bottle of shampoo." I locked eyes with Felipe. "I battled that for nineteen years," he conceded. "You name it, I did it. Heroin. Cocaine. Rocks. Acid. Whatever."

I leaned closer to him. "Really?"

"Yeah, there was a three-year stretch when I lived in my sister's apartment. I lived in the basement, and she never checked on me. I was making six hundred dollars a week, and she never made me pay rent. All my money went to drugs."

Guys like Felipe inspired me to learn more about homelessness in the first place. For most of my life, I overheard off handed comments and jokes about the homeless community and its drug abuse. I hadn't been in an environment where people battled drug use throughout periods of their life, but automatically discounting them never felt right to me. I wanted to understand their pain better. Judging someone by comparing them to my own experience seemed hypocritical and lazy.

Felipe confessed, "I was high on cocaine when my son was being born. I was in the delivery room with my wife, and then I'd go into the bathroom real quick to take a hit of an eight ball. I'd come back again all charged up. 'Come on, honey! You can do this! Come on, baby!' She knew I was high." He shook his head. "I'm sober now," he said with a painful smile. "It's taken a year and a half to get here—counseling, support, rehab. My sister and family have been a big part. It's been extremely challenging. The toughest thing I've done."

The accomplishment of his feat sunk into my mind. Drugs hijacked a person. They controlled the individual. To prioritize a high before the birth of his own child? Felipe had been in deep. "Man, that's hard to believe."

He nodded bashfully. "It got to the point where only turning to God could save me. My preacher says I have conviction now—that I have a purpose and a reason to stop."

"That's a pretty good thing to have, hey?" People searched their whole lives for purpose. It was a human instinct: to believe there was a reason for their existence and that their struggles were not in vain.

"Uh huh." He bobbed his head. "The thought of heroin repulses me now. I get sick." He grimaced. "With drugs, you can get this phlegm cough—some of the guys here have it. They say it's only a cold, but it's definitely from heroin. The crashes and withdrawals are so bad that guys will have to be strapped down to a table so everything clears out of their system."

"Oh my God," I gasped. I exhaled and rolled my shoulders. I pictured a man tied down in a hospital bed, screaming for help. My heart ached.

"Whenever I passed a spot where I knew someone was selling, my body craved it. I had to stop and buy it," he said, clutching his forearm. "I got arrested one time for buying three bags of heroin. The dealer had at least thirty more bags on him. He ran and the cops chased after him."

"Holy cow." My eyebrows shot up. Felipe had *really* been in deep. I tried to understand that feeling—the lack of control—something else ruling my body and decisions. It scared me.

"When smoking crack, you see this sparkle when you light the pipe. When you inhale, you start to fly!" He fluttered his arms, imitating a bird. "Crack gives you a longer high than cocaine. Weed is nothing—it's not addicting." He flipped his hand. "And crystal meth can be made here in the US, so it's cheaper than crack. It doesn't have to be imported."

I nodded. "Damn, man. I had no clue about all that and how tough it is to kick." I shook my head and wiped my heavy eyes. "Thanks for sharing that, man. I'm proud of you." I put my arm on his shoulder. "Keep it up, Felipe. You're not alone." I flashed a sad smile.

"Thanks for the support. Every bit helps, you know   just reaffirms," he said.

"On another note: I can't imagine you on cocaine." I nudged him. "You're already like the Energizer Bunny—standing over my mat in the morning, mocking me for not being a morning person."

Felipe let go of the solemn face and smiled enormously. "It's just who I am. Try to keep up!" he jabbed. I matched his smile with a huge one of my own.

Journal Entry — October 25, 2011

I've decided to leave Inspired Horizons and Rawls on November 10. My gut tells me I need to move on. I wanted to know how living homeless felt, and I'm pretty much there. Yes, I feel like I've stopped learning new things. And yes, especially during the last few weeks, I've felt my psychological health decline from the burden of living homeless. But it's from my friends that I've realized I need to leave.

Some of my friends left already, including Elias. Some I see sporadically so I don't really know if they've gotten something better. But if I don't see them, it's probably a good sign. Living in the shelter is the only place where friends look each other in the eye and say, usually with a laugh, "Well, I hope I never see you again!"

I can feel the attention turn toward me. More and more, guys wonder when I'm going to leave. They care about my situation and want to see me progress and move on. It's like they're putting this subtle pressure on me. It reminds me of high school or college. I came in as a freshman, knowing very little about the culture and system. The upperclassmen guided me, but they eventually left. Now it's my turn to graduate.

Thanksgiving is in a month, and I want to experience it homeless. After thinking about my conversation with Pete and Reggie about going to bars to intentionally meet women, hoping to find a place to crash, I decided I'm going to try it. November 10 is an arbitrary date. But it's on a Thursday, a night many choose to spend like a weekend, which I think increases my chances of success. And if I can leave Inspired Horizons and Rawls one day earlier, I'm going to do it. It's crushing me. After that, I'm going to wing it until Thanksgiving, like I did my first month. I guess I'll see how it goes.

CHAPTER TWENTY-FOUR

CRYING OVER SPILLED MILK

It was morning. The rain outside exaggerated the Inspired Horizons yellow lights inside the cafeteria. I stared down at my tray. It wasn't right—just like everything had become. A number of factors contributed to my increasing depression, but the most recent was from spending the previous night as a Viking, a new nickname at Rawls for those whose beds lay in the expanded, flooded area; it was all anyone could do to help alleviate the thought of waking up, floating in a newly formed sea. The morning process stayed the same: each person dragged their mat to the storage room and hurled it on top of all the others. Whether someone slept on a wet mat the next night was a matter of chance. The lack of sanitation spiraled out of control.

Trying to sleep was a challenging game of Twister. I contorted my body in awkward positions to keep dry. My flexibility and muscular stamina eventually gave out, so I dug into my backpack for a T-shirt and socks to lie on the wet spots. They became so irreversibly disgusting by the time Andre's voice rang that I threw them in the garbage and crossed myself to honor their sacrifice.

The cold and rainy clouds squashed any hint of happy thoughts. They mandated me to sit alone at breakfast as punishment for my unknown crimes, and I obeyed. I was gloom manifested. While my three bowls of generic-brand corn flakes and dry Starbucks cranberry scone only looked staler than usual, the manila-colored milk in my Styrofoam cup was certainly spoiled. Small yellow chunks floated to the surface.

I picked it up and squinted, wondering how it passed for serving. I brought it to my nose and sniffed. *Woof!* I set the cup back down and stared at it with a frown.

A faded-green tray banged in front of me.

Clack!

I didn't look up.

"Hey, Rick," said a voice I recognized as Clyde's. "How you doin'?" he asked in his commanding yet monotone voice.

"I'm all right, you know?" I replied instinctively.

"No. How you *really* doin'?" he demanded. My head shot up, and I straightened my back. No one had ever confronted me for a mundane, small-talk response. Clyde meant it—he actually wanted to know how I was doing. "Have you found an apartment yet?"

"Um. Well. I think I'm gonna be outta here by mid-November," I answered.

"Why not the beginning of November?" he prodded deeper.

I felt off-balanced—a dizziness shot to my head. "I'm looking to go back home in Wisconsin. I think as the holidays get closer, my mom will want me back."

Clyde nodded, straight-lipped.

I rotated my tray to bring the scone closer but accidentally knocked over the cup of sour milk. "Ah!" I cried. The milk drenched my hoodie sleeves, jeans, and the floor below me.

I hung my head and sighed heavily. The cold milk seeped through my clothes. My combination of internal anger and apathy numbed my ability to take action. I continued sitting and did nothing but stare painfully at my tray.

Finally, I stood up and plodded to the garbage can. I dumped all my uneaten food and clumsily placed my tray unevenly onto the others. One by one, I plucked napkins by the kitchen window and returned to my seat.

I wiped the milk from the table surface, then tossed a handful of napkins on the ground, and lazily swung my shoe back and forth.

"I gotta go, Clyde."

"Okay," he said. I gathered my stuff, winced with every movement as I felt my wet clothes against my skin, and shuffled to the exit.

"Hola!" Rita waved to me when I entered the Mor-Way Laundromat doors. I flashed her a half-hearted smile and marched to the cracked, faded-red plastic chairs bolted down to the floor, setting down my overfilled backpack. As I began carefully removing my arm from the milk-soaked hoodie sleeve, she brought me a large white towel from a side room.

"*Gracias.*" I nodded with a puffed face, swollen from anguish.

She smiled. "*De nada.*"

For the last two months, Rita and I saw each other every week and a half. She was a young, plump Mexican woman with rosy cheeks. She had a cheery eagerness. The first time I met her, I explained that I wanted to wash everything I had in one load. I wanted her permission before stripping down to only my red swim trunks and flip-flops. The idea made her giggle, but rather than balk at the idea of my waiting shirtless, she lent me a towel to cover my bare upper body. Her gesture made me feel welcomed and cared for. I looked forward to laundry days.

After dumping all my clothes into the washer and spreading a box of fifty-cent detergent, I dragged myself to a chair. Cold air blustered through the poorly insulated storefront window behind me. I hugged the towel tightly around my shoulders and waited anxiously.

Ding! The washing machine time expired. I rose from my seat. The forced movement helped my blood circulate. I carried the armful of clothes to a dryer with an open door, sloppily stuffing everything inside. I dropped the quarters into the slots. They clanked together at the bottom. The task was half-completed. I sauntered back to my seat.

"Ahhhh!" I screamed in sudden pain. I stubbed my toe on the metal post connected to the seat.

Rita looked up from across the room and watched me hop in circles on one foot, shrieking in agony. She ran over to me.

"*Estas bien?*" she asked. I was too caught up to respond. She looked down at my foot. "Ohh!" she gasped with wide eyes. She turned and headed back. Her reaction confirmed my first terrifying thought: my toe was bleeding.

I looked down, then jerked right back up. A flap of skin barely held on while blood gushed past. Nausea struck instantly. My mouth gaped for oxygen. The sight of blood shocked me into a state of wooziness, but images of the unsanitary conditions at Rawls blinded me.

"*Aqui! Aqui!*" Rita urged. She shoved five bandages into my hand and gripped my shoulder to stabilize my wobbling body. I felt her pulse rapidly vibrate.

She guided me step-by-step to the closet-sized bathroom and helped me splash water on the toe. She realized I couldn't focus enough on my own, so she grabbed two bandages from my hand, unwrapped one, and handed it to me to wrap my toe. It required a second, so she unwrapped the next one. She stepped back. Her hand pressed her red cheek.

"*Bueno? Beuno?*" she fired. I nodded quietly, leaning my hand on the bathroom doorway for balance. I felt like I failed to show her how much I truly appreciated her aid. She tended to me when I didn't have the ability myself, like other homeless individuals. I would've had to deplete my already-low funds to walk to the nearest store to buy a bandage, all while blood spewed like a fountain from my toe.

"*Bueno,*" I mumbled. I wondered if the injury itself caused her reaction, or if she could sense I was burned out and on the verge of a psychological collapse. Either way, I appreciated how she handled my fragility. Kindness meant a lot to the homeless. It humanized situations; it showed empathy and understanding. Kindness was a nonphysical hug, which was always needed.

Journal Entry — October 28, 2011

I'm pushing my psychological limits to the boundary. This next week and a half is going to be so extraordinarily tough. Before, my goal was far away, so my mindset was that I needed to just keep going and it'd eventually come. Now I know the date and it's so hard to focus on one day at a time. It feels like waves crashing into me. I try to take a slight mental rest, but time presses on and doesn't wait. I'll be okay for a couple hours, but then another wave swallows me. There are no breaks when homeless. I feel totally burned out right now. I'm tired and don't feel well. It's like I can't breathe. I'm existing but not living.

CHAPTER TWENTY-FIVE

HELP THE HOMELESS

A thunder of noise blitzed the train car. A thin man stepped inside from the emergency exit behind me and shut the door behind him. The loud distraction vanished like it had been sucked by a vacuum.

He gave me a sup nod. He knew right away and pointed to my shirt. "You didn't do the polar plunge, did you?"

"Nope." I smiled back. "Not sure where I got this." I looked down, pinching my long-sleeved T-shirt out.

The man moved forward to the middle of the L car. A backpack hung from his shoulder, and he had a notebook and folder in his hand. The train car was abnormally full for a late Sunday morning but kept its laidback vibe. He took a deep breath. His chest rose. His feet stood shoulder-width apart, providing a stable foundation for an unpredictable ride. He projected his voice.

"Hey, everyone." He rotated his body. "My name is Tatum. I was just released from prison." He held up a laminated copy of his profile and record. He scanned for eye contact to deliver a more personalized message.

The situation reminded me of my social psychology class in college. Tatum excused my participation on the account of homelessness. It allowed me to observe, and the reactions fascinated me. Some, when aware what was going on, joined everyone else with their heads locked downward. No one made eye contact. No one said anything. They knew the drill. This scenario was common in Chicago. The car became eerily still.

He continued, "Does anyone have any job information or money to help me buy a thirty-day CTA pass?" He paused, hoping for a verbal response from someone—anyone. "I'm doing my best, and I don't want to steal. I would appreciate it if someone could help me." I knew how valuable a thirty-day pass was. It allowed me to travel anywhere I wanted in the city, as much as I needed. Every month, it was my first priority. Travel was an overlooked issue among the homeless—travel to resources, travel to their job, travel to family, and, most frustrating of all, travel to and from bureaucratic agencies where progress of their situation moved at a snail-like pace.

Crickets.

"If you have anything—*anything*—it would help out a lot," he pleaded. He waited, deflating like a balloon. The stone-faced men and women also waited . . . for him to finish and try his luck in the next train car.

Some passengers looked to others to step up; if another acted, they'd certainly help too. Each person had been conditioned to ignore his existence. A couple questions might've passed through their heads. I used to imagine them myself. *How do I know if he really needs help, or even if he's telling the truth? If I help this individual, will it encourage begging in the future—isn't that bad for society? What if I offer to help the stranger and put myself in harm's way?*

But no one tried to get answers. No one asked follow-up questions. Conformity ruled. The fear of being labeled a *sucker* influenced them more than one man's gratitude.

I sucked in my lips and watched Tatum stump to the emergency exit. He rotated the handle, and the loud screech of grinding rails surged into the car. Silence returned when he stepped out and shut the door behind him.

"Who was that, Dad?" a toddler asked his father.

He shook his head. "Don't worry about it."

Journal Entry — October 30, 2011

I've seen a lot of people in the past two and half months begging for money. I remember one day seeing a young child and her mother sitting on the ground, holding a sign reading HOMELESS. NEED HELP. My perception and ideas have evolved.

I don't think anyone needs to be sitting on the street begging. I think there are enough resources in Chicago, at least, to get someone started in the right direction—but then I wonder if these people know about them. From what I've seen, it's a chaotic mess. Others know better than me, like Elias, who tried every day to improve his situation. He expressed his frustration a lot. In that case, I guess I can't fault them for begging.

Originally, I thought I'd need to beg for money. I imagined it'd just be something I had to do, whether I liked it or not. I delayed because I thought it'd be humiliating. Once I entered the shelter, I realized few people actually begged. Being homeless doesn't mean having absolutely nothing. Guys get income in various ways. It depends on each situation. Some get social security or disability; some have jobs; some have to be more creative because their limited formal education and criminal records prevent them from getting jobs that society deems real. One guy took a pay cut to hand out flyers to people because, "You never know who you're going to meet—maybe Donald Trump will walk by one day. Opportunity isn't going to walk into the dayroom and hand you a job."

I only know two guys who beg: Luis and Farouk. They're good at it. That's their job. Farouk told me he typically begs downtown from 6:00 a.m. to 1:00 p.m., or 7:00 a.m. to 2:00 p.m. But neither of them use the method I usually see—they don't waste their time holding a sign and looking sad to coax pity from passersby. They walk right up to people with their hand out, which Luis told me is illegal.

"I've been put in jail four times for doing it already. They put you in jail, you eat, and take a nap for four hours. Then they let you go and give you a court date, but you don't go to it, though. They're not going to put out a warrant for you."

I'm skeptical and suspicious of people on the street appearing hopeless and helpless, sitting silently with a sign. But on the other hand, I get it. They're free. They don't have to confront the faceless tyranny of the homeless shelter and its suffocating structure and rules. They don't have to wake up at a certain time, eat breakfast at a certain time, be at roll call at a certain time, or be at a shelter at a certain time. If they're begging for money, they're more reliant on the generosity of strangers, but they're more independent as a whole. If you want to use the available resources, your freedom is the tradeoff.

Of all the homeless people I've come across so far, no one is like these people sitting on the corner with a sign, sulking in misery. It's those posers who exaggerate their body language to reap sympathy from the uncomfortable public who give society its ideas of homelessness. This small population has become the representation of an entire community.

CHAPTER TWENTY-SIX

ON EDGE

Clyde nudged me. I could only rotate my head. We packed the van like sardines in a can, largely with guys unfamiliar to me.

"I went to the Laundromat, and a guy was shot."

My head jolted forward. "You serious?"

"Yeah. I saw a body layin' there in a puddle of blood, and then when I walked out, I just saw some yellow tape in the area."

The man behind us interjected. "Oh, yeah, you know there finna be a few shootings over by Rawls tonight," he declared. "It's Halloween. One outta three guys is probably carryin'."

My stomach felt knotted from nervousness. I turned back to Clyde. "You're talkin' about the Laundromat at Sunnyside and Sheridan, right? By the pawn shop and Chinese place?"

"Yeah," he confirmed. "The one we get tokens for."

"The fuck! See! That's why I don't go there. You guys are always like, 'Rick, just go to the Laundromat off Sunnyside. Lenny will help you out.' That's why!" I said. Clyde shrugged his shoulders a tiny bit.

Our reactions differed vastly. A dead body was nothing to Clyde, yet it threw me into a panic. Perhaps when he was young and half his weight, gun violence frightened him like it did me. He grew numb to it over the course of his life. After almost three months, my awareness of the issue increased significantly. But I failed to determine whether it made me more numb or piled onto my mounting stress—the latter was a stronger bet.

"Phil, you know about the flooding, right?" someone voiced to the driver's seat.

"Yeah, you fellas talk about it. There's some leak or some shit?" Phil recalled.

"It ain't just a leak no more. It's a goddamned flood!" the man seethed. "Guys wake up swimmin' for their lives." Groans congested the air inside the van.

"It's the sewage pipe!" someone proclaimed.

"Nah, man. It's the water main," someone else corrected him. "Well, no one knows, but that's my guess. It'd smell worse if it was the sewage." Heads bobbed in agreement. "Either way, Rawls ain't sanitary. Horizons has gotta cut off the contract. It's inhumane." The chatter grew louder.

A man said, "Horizons used to have a contract with a different shelter, but the sanitary conditions got so bad that they went to Rawls."

"Well, Horizons won't have to make that decision. The city's gonna do it for them! No way Rawls is still open in a month! I'd bet two thousand dollars."

"You ain't got a *thousand* dollars, man!"

"Well, if I did, it'd be the easiest way to double my money. Be sure about that," he said.

Of all the issues at Rawls, the flooding was the tipping point for most guys. Nothing was done to fix a problem that left the floor of a homeless shelter underwater. It violated the trust of the men. Clearly, the shelter didn't care enough about the safety—but more so the dignity—of vulnerable individuals. Everyone seemed on edge, including me.

———

Clyde, Juan, and I waited together along the kitchen wall. Volunteers had just stored the tables underneath the stage and had begun sweeping. A man near us watched a horror movie on a portable DVD player.

Juan recalled, "I remember when *The Exorcist* came out. I went and saw it in the theaters, and I wasn't okay for like a week." He laughed with a hitch. "That was probably the scariest movie I've seen. I don't watch many, though."

"Yeah, I don't like scary movies, either," Clyde admitted. "That stuff freaks me out." It was hard to imagine a scared Clyde. He looked so intimidating.

"Same here," I agreed. "But not as much when I watch the old scary movies. I don't know. The sets and effects are so bad." Clyde and Juan nodded.

"The scariest ones are the mind ones"—Juan touched his head—"those ones age better. They mess with your head."

"They should make a movie about this article I read recently," Clyde noted. "There's these Satanic priests in small towns in Texas. Everybody's normal during the day, and then at night, they all get together, worship the devil, and perform fucked-up rituals," he described. "They'll befriend out-of-towners, and then rape them." Juan and I stared at Clyde with frozen faces. "I ain't ever goin' to Texas!"

At a quicker pace than normal, volunteers finished sweeping and some hauled mats out.

A man with a balding head stood seven feet in front of us, boxing an imaginary foe, throwing jabs into the air. "Didn't see that comin', did you?" he mumbled. Discolored patches covered his sleeveless arm. He had gross, crusty skin. His fingers didn't move; they looked locked in place in various positions, some straight and some bent.

Clyde leaned toward him. "You're bleeding on your leg."

The disoriented man turned to Clyde but didn't speak.

Clyde pointed down. "Your leg! It's bleeding!"

The man returned to his boxing in a nonchalant manner.

Clyde's face pinched together, and he stood up. "Hey! Your leg!" Clyde called, just shy of yelling.

"Whoa, whoa, whoa!" The pudgy substitute manager jogged over, out of breath. "What's going on here?"

"He's spewing like a waterfall! He's just standing there doing nothing, letting himself bleed!"

The manager gestured to Clyde to calm down. Others looked to our direction. Hisses rumbled. The bleeding man silently watched Clyde and the manager, his arms limped at his side.

"I saw him scratching his body in the shower earlier too," Clyde said. "Something can spread."

"Yeah, he's right!" someone near us shouted.

The manager waved his hand to the bleeding man. "Here, come with me." He followed him past Clyde, standing like a statue except for his staring eyes.

The manager approached someone sitting in a chair next to the kitchen door. "You mind if I use this chair?"

The previously unaware person jumped off his chair, trying to avoid the bleeding man who took his place. The manager walked into the kitchen. Guys huddled around each other, whispering intensely, and glared to the kitchen door.

The manager walked back out of the kitchen with a handful of paper towels and told the man to wipe the blood. No bandages or disinfectant materials were used—just water and paper towels. The manager didn't call the police or ask for help outside of the shelter. He didn't go above the call of duty. He skated by with minimal effort applied to the situation. The quiet conversations erupted into boisterous noises.

"That guy could have leprosy!" a man called from the center of the room.

"Or syphilis!" another shouted.

"Man, he's putting us all at risk to get AIDS or some shit!" someone else yelled.

Juan and I witnessed Clyde's frustration grow like ours. We sensed the heat emitting from his fuming body. Veins bulged from his neck. An anxious energy festered in the room from the worriedness from each person.

"He didn't even get a Band-Aid. He needs to go to the hospital!" the same man near us barked.

"If the cops were here, they wouldn't hesitate," another angry voice said.

The way the substitute manager handled the situation infuriated me, and I was convinced that if Andre had been present, it wouldn't have escalated. Andre wasn't lazy. It was the most serious event I experienced at Rawls. Panic boiled inside my body, hijacking my consciousness. I took deep breaths, hoping more oxygen would cure my dizziness. I focused not on Clyde, the bleeding man, or the roars of anger around me, but on regaining control of my body.

The previously bleeding man lay alone. The manager isolated his mat along the kitchen wall, away from everyone else, hoping to quell the men's rage. No one was fooled. Everyone knew the mats were never washed. The concerned faces around me wondered if they'd sleep on that same mat on another night. I worried too.

Clyde's mat was next to mine in the center of the room. He said, "You look around and the volunteers all get their own mats and bleach spray, but we get nothing to clean ours with. That's what happens when you let cons run places, Rick." I sulked. I didn't know what else to say. The night still processed in my head. "I'm gonna get my own place in a few days. I'm supposed to get a check so you can stay with me if you want. I'll be getting high—and I know you don't do that—but at least you'll get away from this stuff for a bit. You can chill and relax. If I stay here much longer, I'm gonna go crazy and snap." He shook his head.

I thanked him, and Clyde's body hit the mat. Felipe fixed his bed on the other side of me.

The lights flicked off. I lay on my back, thinking about everything that happened. Suddenly, faintness rushed through me. I flipped over and shot to my knees and gagged, feeling like I was about to vomit. My hands tingled sharply. I looked over my shoulder at the bathroom area, quickly planning my route. It became too much.

I jumped from my mat and paced toward the bathroom, covering my mouth just in case.

It was the only time I was glad the middle stall had no door. I charged right to the stained toilet, bent over, and spewed fluids and chunks from my mouth. *The hell!* I shook my head in disbelief.

I lurched forward again but dry-heaved; a long strand of drool hung from my mouth until it touched the toilet. I pulled back and leaned my hand against the graffiti-covered wall. Tears of relief streamed from the corners of my eyes.

I returned to my mat and lay down. I closed my eyes.

"Tomorrow's a new day, guys!" someone yelled.

My God, I needed to hear that. Everyone needed to hear that.

Journal Entry — October 31, 2011

The shitty weather, constant talk of gangs and violence, and being homeless in general put pressure on
me all the time. It's always there. I can't escape it.
They chip more and more at my psyche; every situation
heightens my anxiety. I'm not doing well. It's so
fucking hard not to focus on the negative.

That being said, there was one positive tonight—one that I'll never forget. During the
whole debacle, when people shouted different
diseases instead of saying shingles, someone
said *jingles*. I turned to Clyde, who was as serious as ever, and joked in my stupid game show
host voice.

"Look out! He's got *the jingles*!"

Clyde laughed so hard that he literally bent
over and slapped his knees. "He's got the jingles—that's hilarious." It was only the second
time I've seen him smile or laugh. For as fucked
up as tonight was, that moment made me happy.

And that's all I needed.

CHAPTER TWENTY-SEVEN

KEEP WALKING

Juan's new cane made him appear older. He leaned it against his chair. We waited in the shower line together. His ankle hadn't improved. Weariness replaced the twinkle in his eyes.

"I think I'm going to focus on salvation," he confessed.

"Yeah?" I said. Both of us carefully rested our tiptoes on the flooded floor.

He nodded. "I've been doing more reflecting lately. And, you know, being here has accelerated that." I crossed my arms and rested my hand on my bearded chin. I leaned back in the chair. "But I think salvation is reached by being a good person and doing good things."

"Well, I think you're a good person, Juan. And remember you shared Hershey bars with our table about a week back? That probably shot you up God's wait list a few spots." I nudged him.

"Oh, yeah, I'm right up there with Mother Theresa," he mocked.

"See, that's the spirit!" I mirrored his sarcasm. Juan's smile vanished. He slid his hand over his bald head. He focused outward to the rest of the room.

"I don't agree a lot with the guys here. It seems like they make up theologies to fit with their life," Juan concluded.

I frowned. "Mhm."

Juan gripped my arm tightly. "I mean, Rick, some of these guys think the devil himself is making them do things. They don't take control of their own lives. They're waiting for God to rescue them, but he's not."

"I've noticed that with some," I said.

"It's not *some*, Rick. It's a lot. Their spirituality gets in their own way. It shouldn't be like that. You look around and think of all the problems these guys have . . ." Juan elbowed me hard. "Look!" He scanned the room with his finger. "Alcoholism. Drug addiction. Mental illnesses. Most have little education—I mean, you've seen when we sign in, it takes some guys five minutes to write their name. And when there's a problem, it takes nine people to solve it. There's a lot of issues, and their spirituality should help them, not keep them down."

I nodded and stared soberly at Juan. "Yeah, I know."

Juan paused and breathed slower. "I'll get into Section 8 housing soon," he said. "I just need a note from my doctor, which shouldn't be too hard. I'm in physical therapy now for my ankle."

"That's good, man."

"Well, I just hope they don't put me on the south side—anywhere but there!" Juan laughed nervously.

I matched his laugh with a smile. "I feel ya. I don't think I'd do well there, either. What's the first thing you're going to do when you get a place?"

"Take a hot bath." Juan laughed. "And lay in there for hours with no one yelling at me."

"Oooooh! Yeah, that's a great idea."

"And I'm going to have a *whole* towel," he said.

"Now you're talkin'!"

I threw my backpack on a chair next to Marquis.

"Hey, Jesus!" Farouk laughed from across the table. Jesus was his new nickname for me because of my ever-growing beard. I understood the context, but it made me nervous around other guys, especially spiritual ones. I didn't want to be associated with blasphemy.

I joined them in the middle of their conversation about Farouk's citizenship. He'd been in the US for ten years and said he had no ID.

"But if I marry my girlfriend, I'll be a citizen," Farouk said.

"How do you pay your lawyer, Farouk?" Marquis asked.

"I have *two* lawyers!" Farouk corrected Marquis.

Marquis smiled and shook his head. Marquis seemed to be in a good mood. He still moved slowly, but he had a buoyancy I hadn't seen from him. "How do you like the other Nigerians at Horizons?" he asked Farouk.

"I don't like them—only a few." Farouk's demeanor flipped. He stared at Marquis, like he was angry Marquis asked. Marquis and I jerked our heads back. We'd never seen Farouk show any hostility.

There must've been some bad blood between Farouk and the other Nigerians—a story Marquis and I didn't know about.

"Okay, okay. Sorry to ask." Marquis waved his hands.

Farouk quickly snapped back into his fun-loving self. He pulled Powerball tickets from his coat. "If I win, I'll give you a thousand dollars, Jesus!" he pledged.

I grinned, stroking my beard. "I'mma hold you to it."

"You should comb your beard," he demanded. "It's really, really bushy."

"I'm undecided what I should do with it yet," I said.

Farouk leaned his body over the table and tugged on it. I sat still to limit any pain. "It feels weird." He laughed. "I couldn't keep that on my face."

"Farouk, you can't grow a beard," Marquis teased.

Farouk spun his head to him. "Hey!" Marquis and I smiled. Farouk rotated his whole body back to me. "I wanna see you walk on water."

"Nah. If I'm pullin' any miracles, I'm going to turn that water"—I pointed to the water fountain across the room—"into wine." Farouk burst into laughter so hard it turned to a wheezing cough. He bent his head down and put his hand on his stomach to control himself. Hanging with Farouk made the time pass quicker. He was a lovable guy.

I stepped out of the bathroom and took a deep breath of fresher air, toothbrush in hand.

Vinny, near the small set of stairs, paced back and forth with an irritated focus. He held his phone to his ear. I crept to him, trying to eavesdrop as much as possible. His fiancée called off the marriage.

"If you saw any of my other brothers, and the way they treat their wives, you'd be blown away. That's how I was raised—to always be nice and treat a woman well," he pleaded to his would-be mother-in-law. Vinny continued on the phone, pitching why he'd be a good husband. I couldn't say I was surprised Vinny's fiancée had second thoughts, but I felt bad for him. His upcoming marriage gave him a date to look forward to. Positivity now required more searching. It made me think of Pete and how he would've reacted when I told him. Pete got a place a couple days earlier. The news wouldn't have shocked him, either.

I returned to my chair along the kitchen wall. Volunteers mopped the floor in the center of the room. Clyde appeared even bluer than usual.

"I was at my sister's, and the check didn't come. I talked to the social security officer on the phone and, while I was on hold, my brother-in-law told me it was taken care of, and that I didn't need to talk to them."

"Oh." I leaned a little closer to hear his monotone murmur.

"My brother-in-law is my payee. He's responsible for makin' sure I'm doin' all right 'cause of my mental condition," Clyde explained. "If he took my check, I'll either get him in jail because he was messin' with my money, or I'll go over there and break every single window on their house and car. I'll go back to jail. They don't work hard. They're lazy and I can't stand lazy people." I nodded, listening intently. "They're all talk. I'll try to make my sister laugh or something by poking fun at myself or my addiction, but she's just sour-faced all the time."

"Oh." His comment momentarily distracted me. Clyde wasn't a jubilant person. I only saw him laugh twice since I met him.

"I swear, Rick, yesterday, I was walking down the street, and I just wanted to keep walking. I wanted to keep walking until I didn't know where I was." He sighed heavily, exhausted from life's obstacles. "I wish I had your family."

My head bowed. I didn't have a response for him.

Clyde worried me. His addiction was one thing, but his deeper issues troubled me more. I knew what he truly wanted—and so did he. He wanted desperately to escape the life he knew, and all that came with it. He wanted to start over somewhere else, and he was more than capable of doing it. But Clyde was afraid. And his fear of the unknown controlled him. It saddened me, knowing he'd give in to his prescribed fate. I could tell just by looking at his fatigued body. Starting over required energy Clyde no longer had.

Journal Entry — November 5, 2011

I really don't know how to put this. It sounds fucked up, but I feel like two people: Rich and Rick. I don't know if it stems back to looking at the dead twin that early Sunday morning or what. I've thought more about the idea of souls since then. It's like Rich is my spirit, my heart, and my mind. And Rick is human. Rich wants to learn and explore different perspectives, but he's using Rick to do it—his human body.

Rich recently realized that he's immortal and that everything is only limited to how far he can imagine; but unfortunately, it's at Rick's expense. Rich is pushing him too hard, beyond his boundaries. Rich even knows it, but he flat out doesn't care. He's going to continue regardless of Rick's deteriorating well-being. In fact, part of Rich is fascinated by how far Rick has crashed; seeing him on the cusp of a psychological breakdown piques his curiosity. By putting Rick through this, Rich learns more and more about deep human emotions that were once foreign to him. Rick bears the brunt of living homeless and everything that goes with it. And it's like Rich now is mainly preoccupied with analyzing Rick instead of Rick's friends at the shelter.

But it's really only when typing the journal entries that Rich comes out—Rick's thoughts dominate every time besides then. It's like I

can remove myself from my body and see what's
happening to Rick. It's like this incredibly unhealthy tug-of-war that's happening in my head.
I don't know who will win—or if anyone will win.

CHAPTER TWENTY-EIGHT

IT WAS ALL WORTH IT

"Wait for me, Rick. I'm coming with you." Juan stood above my mat, holding his cane. I opened my case and put my glasses on. The lights hadn't been on for more than two minutes.

"Yeah? You know you've said that the last four nights," I jabbed.

"Well, this time I mean it," he said.

I reached for my shoes at the end of my mat. "All right. Let's meet by the stairs."

"Okay." He hobbled to his mat ten feet away. He hadn't started collecting his things. I glanced at my left wrist. There was no chance we'd catch the 5:56 bus.

"Hey, take your time, Juan."

"Oh. Okay," he answered like a confused old man.

We finally made it onto the northbound bus to Inspired Horizons. The whole process, walking to the bus stop and transferring, took longer than normal. I didn't mind, though; I always enjoyed Juan's company, and we'd still be on time for breakfast.

"You know, the city really went downhill in the fifties." Juan's grouchy mood gurgled up some of his dim views of the future. "After World War II, all the money moved out to the suburbs—my aunt saw it herself 'cause she's been here since the twenties."

"Yeah, that makes sense. That was the American Dream, right? To own a house, cars, and have a backyard for all your kids to enjoy?"

Juan nodded. "Mhm. Everything was cookie-cutter mass-produced. But it really hurt the cities," Juan said. "Employers used to walk down the street and give jobs to anyone who wanted one. It wasn't like that after so many people left. And it's certainly not like that now!" he proclaimed. He crossed his arms. "With fewer economic opportunities, neighborhoods collapsed. Take the neighborhood Rawls is in for example: you think that area was always like that? No. Of course not. But throughout time, all these factors impact it."

And with dwindled economic opportunities, people found it more difficult to afford housing. Everything was connected: politics, race, religion, education, economics, healthcare, crime, culture shifts, etc. It made my head dizzy thinking about it. Day after day, the traditional stereotype of a homeless person seemed more ludicrous and naïve to me. It discounted the histories of all these issues and how it affected generations and generations of people in America. There was no solution for homelessness. For an optimist like myself, that's hard to swallow, but it was true.

Juan grabbed my arm and focused on my eyes. "We're not headed in the right direction." He shook his head. "It's so hard for people to afford the cost of living. If you're not making at least fifteen dollars an hour, you're going to struggle. Depending on social security isn't enough."

"Social security won't even be a thing when I'm old," I said.

"I don't think so, either." Juan hung his head. He knew the financial burden younger generations inherited from their predecessors.

"The national debt is fourteen trillion dollars." I raised my voice. "Who do you think will have to solve that problem?"

"Not me." Juan waved, shaking his head like his mouth was zipped shut.

"Exactly!" I felt my heartbeat increase.

Juan urged, "What the government should do is tax big businesses more, but they won't because they let 'em push 'em around. Politicians give them handouts. Lobbyists own them." The term *handouts* was usually affiliated with poor Americans and the homeless. It was one of the first times I heard it used to describe businesses and politicians.

I stroked my beard. "Yeah, I don't know." I sighed. "I don't think taxing is always the answer. It's too easy, too lazy."

"It's greed, Rick. A lot of money is at the top and it doesn't come down like they say it does. You saw those people outside when we passed the Reserve, right? They've been there a month, saying the same thing I just said."

I groaned. "I know. I know." A movement called Occupy Wall Street swept the nation since I had become homeless. It started in New York but spread to other cities, including Chicago. Each morning, on the bus ride back to Inspired Horizons, I passed protestors camped on the sidewalk. Coverage of it dominated the news and conversations among strangers. I agreed with its sentiment but found myself confused by its goals—or if it had any. If it only intended to raise awareness that 1 percent of the American population controlled most of the wealth of the country, they succeeded. But to me, that seemed like a low bar. Anyone who picked up an American history book could figure that out. I learned that statistic in my sixth grade social studies class. Maybe it was too much for Americans to stomach now, especially after the financial crisis, which many got the short end of the stick.

"There's a lot of anger right now," Juan said. "You can feel it. This country's not right." I turned to the window and exhaled. "You've seen how many people are at Horizons and Rawls. They need jobs. They need to be put to work and yet we allow all the illegal aliens to stay."

I turned back to him. "Do you think most of the illegal immigrants are working?"

He nodded. "Yeah, and I think they're taking jobs that others can do."

"Are they working jobs others don't want?" I raised one eyebrow.

"A lot of Americans need a kick in the *behind*!" Juan said. "We've gotten soft and pampered. No one wants to grab a brush and get down on their knees. They think they're too good for it."

I grinned. "That'll be a good part of your speech when you're campaigning for president." Juan chuckled. "So where do you stand on education, Mr. President?"

"Kids don't vote." Juan smirked. I burst into laughter.

"See! That's the answer to all these problems," I said. "We need an overhaul of the education system. But we won't. It'll take too long, and politicians don't have patience to invest in something that'll take a generation to see the fruit." Juan bobbed his head.

If anything, I thought education would help reduce the amount of homelessness. Maybe not for guys at Rawls or Inspired Horizons, but for younger people—to break the cycle that had been stuck on my mind. Better overall education and learned skills could help young individuals broaden their perspectives and increase their ability to find more opportunities. Of course, I was biased as someone who received a liberal arts college education and had been shaped by that experience. But I drew the line, unlike many of my peers who decided to jump into a deeper pool of student loan debt, thinking it'd entice their future employers to hire them. I had homeless friends who managed their money better than them. The difference often came down to initial resources.

Juan grew more serious. "You know, we'd have money for education if we weren't in the Middle East. We didn't learn our lesson from before." I listened as he exhaled painfully. "I was lucky because when I was in the air force, I was stationed somewhere else instead of fighting in Vietnam. I had two friends who went over there. They were big guys"—Juan puffed up his chest—"one was blown up, and the other returned and was never the same. It's really sad, too, because he was always a funny guy."

I dropped my shoulders. I didn't know what to say or how to console him. Suddenly, an attractive young Asian woman hopped on the bus. Juan cheered up. He raised his eyebrows and turned to me.

"Rick, you see her?" He tapped my arm.

I laughed. "Yeah, Juan."

"You should talk to her," he encouraged.

"What? No," I said.

Juan chuckled. "I met a twenty-three-year-old woman at the library the other day. We're going on a date soon." He grinned.

My jaw dropped. "What! I can't even get a date with a twenty-three-year-old," I whined.

He threw his head back with a bellied laugh. "Well, you have to try."

I rolled my eyes, smiling to one side. "You gonna treat her with your Link card?" I teased.

He shook his head. "No, I'm waiting for my social security check. And I told her, 'There's no need to dress up—let's just do casual'"— he elbowed me—"I don't have anything to dress up in." He gripped my arm again, laughing.

We traveled closer and closer to our bus stop.

"All right then, Juan, what advice would you give me for meeting girls these days?"

He paused. "You're going to have to fix up your grizzle there." He pointed to my beard, then rubbed his chin.

"Ha!" I threw my head back. "Yeah, yeah. I know. I think I'm going to get rid of it by Thanksgiving. I think I'm going to get out of here and go back to Wisconsin soon."

Suddenly, joy and excitement beamed on his face. I never saw him so elated. "That's great, Rick! You know, you're a real good guy. Any girl would be lucky to be with you. Find the right one." I started laughing to hide my flattery, but he grabbed my arm yet again and interrupted me. "No, I mean it, Rick. One day, you'll meet someone, and she'll be the luckiest girl in the world."

The corner of my eyes became wet. My body felt weightless and weak all over.

Juan looked out the window. "Is this our stop—Wilson?" he asked.

"Uh, yeah," I replied, still staring at him.

We stepped off the bus. Juan gimped and I followed behind to Inspired Horizons.

"You can benefit from this, Rick. You can see the struggles of people and learn from it—better now than when you're old like me."

"Thanks, Juan."

Journal Entry — November 8, 2011

I was real negative before this morning. I don't know. I was up in the air about my homeless experience. Maybe it's because I've gotten so used to everything. Nothing is surprising or new. I haven't had the opportunity to read my journal, debrief, or even think. It's been eating me alive.

But my conversation with Juan reassured me. I wondered if I'd get to a point like this. Juan gave me one of the greatest compliments I ever received in my life. It came with no motives or strings attached; it was sincere and genuine. All he knows is my character and my core as a human being. It made me proud.

While living homeless, I haven't felt that other homeless men judged me, even though I originally assumed they would. We view each other as human beings. And as human beings, we understand that we want the same things: love, dignity, freedom. It hasn't mattered what clothes I wear, how my hair looks, or what things I have. The only thing that matters is my character and how I treat others. I find it so refreshing. Whatever happened to me the last three months, and whatever will happen after this, it was all worth it.

CHAPTER TWENTY-NINE

ALL ALONE AGAIN

Eternity passed. The day finally arrived: November 10. Butterflies fluttered in my stomach. The redundancy would soon be over. Visions of myself doing cartwheels down the Inspired Horizons hallway flashed through my mind. This was the day I'd regain my freedom—not from homelessness, but the homeless shelter.

I put thought into how I'd leave. I decided not to tell anyone. I remembered what Curtis, who'd been long gone, told me about people dancing in prison before they left. No one liked it. I didn't want to be *that guy*. I figured I'd leave like I came—suddenly and unannounced.

I rose from my mat and performed the same routine from the previous sixty mornings. Each task, I thought how it was the last time. *This is the last time I'll drop my bedsheet into the dirty pile. This is the last time I'll throw my mat into the musty storage room. This is the last time I'll hold my breath and splash water on my face in the bathroom.*

Juan waited by the shelter exit. "Rick, it's like twenty degrees out there."

I felt a tearful smile cross my face. I nodded to him. "Take care, Juan."

He smiled back at me, like any other day. I turned around, pushed the heavy door out, and left.

———

A strange dizziness came over me as I ambled through the hallway to the dayroom. I imagined my face would hurt from a permanent smile, but I experienced a ghostly numbness instead.

"Hey, Jesus!" Farouk laughed as he passed me.

I shook the cobwebs from my head. "Morning, Farouk," I said too late.

I sat alone at a table. The local morning news was on TV, like it had been every morning. I stared at the clock next to it. The clock ticked, second after second. My pulse matched beat by beat, but then sped quicker and quicker.

Forty-four CTA passes were tucked inside my backpack. Four were in my wallet. This was supposed to be the moment where I gave all the cards to my friends, but they weren't there. None of them. Reggie. Clyde. Julius. Marquis. Pete. Luis. Elias. Jarris. None. My butterflies turned into knots. I lifted my heavy body from the chair. There was no point staying in the dayroom.

I stared at the ground, drifting through the alleyway.

"What's up, Rick?"

I looked up. "Hey, Marquis!"

"Where you headed?" he asked, pushing up his glasses.

"Red line."

His head heaved back. "Well, you better get out of here." He laughed. "Good idea entering from Broadway instead of Wilson. Smart."

I nodded with a sad smile. "Hey, do you need any bus passes?" I asked. I reached into my pocket and pulled out my wallet.

"Ah, nah, man. I don't have any money." I shook my head and stuffed four into his hand. "Don't worry about it."

His eyebrows jumped up. He stared at his hand, now holding four bus passes. His body relaxed. "Thank you," he muttered. "If you ever need anything, let me know."

"Thanks." I nodded. "Take care."

We parted, and I immediately regretted not giving him all the passes in my backpack. I don't know what happened. I blanked. I got so caught up in seeing him that I didn't think to just give him them all. I could've trusted him to disperse them to others. I sighed and tried to put it behind me. What was done was done.

I continued down the alleyway and thought about the past two months. I wasn't going back. As I turned the corner, tears trickled down my face. I probably wouldn't see any of my friends again— friends who became an important part of me. And I didn't only lose one friend—I lost everyone in an instant.

I climbed up the Wilson red line steps and waited alone on the rickety platform. When the train arrived, I dragged myself to a window seat. I stared outside, thinking about Inspired Horizons and

Rawls and all the friendships I had made. My chest grew heavy, and tears streamed down my face. The first flurries of winter fell.

Journal Entry — November 10, 2011

I'm so busy crying I didn't notice I'm the only one in the train car. That's never happened to me before. It's eerie. It's provoking my loneliness. There's no one around to distract me from my thoughts and emotions. I can only hear the train screeching against the rails. The emptiness feels like it's taunting me. I feel like the train—empty inside, without a warm soul. I don't know where I'm going, but I'm going anyway. This chapter is over.

I don't understand what's happening. I looked forward to this moment for so long—for what seemed to be forever—but now I'm wondering if I made a mistake. I'm free from the shelter, but I'm still homeless and have no direction. I'm alone. Doing what I did the first month requires so much energy, but I don't know if I have it in me. I'm so exhausted. I'm so worried.

EPILOGUE

I returned home to Wisconsin on December 10, 2011. It didn't go so well being back—that's a whole other story. I often reflected back on that November 10 date. It haunted me, like it was the day where Rich disappeared and Rick moved forward, vulnerable and lonely to the rest of the world.

What helped was reaching out to my friend, known in this book as Elias. He was the only friend whose contact information I had. He once wrote his email address on a torn-off piece of newspaper. I typed it into my journal and sat on it for over two years. He's a bus driver now.

We always meet in coffee shops because I blame him for my coffee addiction. He's somewhat of a coffee connoisseur. Some of my favorite moments were sipping coffee and having conversations with him—or whoever else.

I always look forward to our conversations. We're just two human beings discussing the wonders of life. I view him as a mentor, and he's not afraid to play devil's advocate for decisions I've made.

I haven't reunited with anyone else. They've been tough to find, especially without the last names of a few. But to be honest, I've given half-hearted effort toward it. I feel conflicted. I would love to see them again if I had the chance, but they're also immortalized in my mind. I love them as the flawed individuals they are—part of me is afraid to lose that. I suppose it's a luxurious thought to have, but I know deep down that they don't need me. I imagine I was just a flash in their life, certainly not as impactful as they've been for me. And I know they're doing all right because they have good character.

I've wondered how I can use my experience living homeless to make a positive impact. I'm not an expert on homelessness, and I'm not trying to be that. That wasn't my goal. Amazing people work every day to help homeless individuals improve their situations. I was just really curious about a community of people trying to navigate their way through a pervasive societal problem, and I wanted to learn how they felt. Immersing myself was the best way for me to learn.

When I returned from living homeless, I tried to wrap my head around everything, but it was like a puzzle whose pieces didn't fit. My experience didn't match with society's ideas of homelessness. It wasn't black and white. It was gray and complex. For the first time, admittedly, I looked up the definition of *homeless*, and it all clicked: *Homeless: individuals lacking permanent housing.* There is no one true homeless experience. Each person has a different story and perspective to share.

If you take anything from this book, I want you to know the

definition of *homeless*. I want you to think more critically about how we use the word. It's the simplest thing you can do for the community. By understanding the actual definition, it's clear that it's highly vague and all-encompassing. There's a wide spectrum of people who fit under *homeless*. Without redefining the word, society's dangerous, stereotyped image prevails and looms over individuals, which, I would argue, causes more detriment than lacking housing itself. Redefine homeless. Visit redefinehomeless.com for more information.

ACKNOWLEDGMENTS

I'd like to thank my family, especially Mom and Dad. Peter and Jess, Emily and Matt, and Dennis. I know this time wasn't easy, but I appreciate your support and love. I'm blessed to have you all. Thank you to Remington Tonar and Benjamin Johnson, the only two besides my parents who knew about this project.

Thank you to all my friends I met during my time living homeless. I'm humbled to know you all. I'm sorry I omitted some of you from this book, but I still love you and appreciate the time we spent together. You inspire me.

To all those experiencing homelessness, or who have experienced it, you are not alone. Stay strong, persistent, and hopeful. Homelessness does not define who you are or your capabilities.

Thank you to all the people who have dedicated their time, careers, and lives to those experiencing homelessness. I understand how difficult it can be and how often your effort is overlooked. Just know—even though it's not said enough—there are many individuals who appreciate your labor.

Thank you to Lorian Sanders, Joe Anhalt, Jhoanny Urbina, Kevin

Bestor, Nick McMillan, Brandon Donovan, Colin Russ, Eddie Groberski, Coreen Wintering, Aneesa Ahmed, Caelin Niehoff, Jason Knoespel, Nate Gilanyi, Tom Neave, Kevin Mueller, Mike Hickey, Nadine Geary, Alex Ngo, Binti Patel, Nick Sunderland, Matt Zimmerman, Dave Kurhajec, Gerald Sorce, Adam Kaprelian, and Travis Backes.

Thank you to everyone who asked me about my homeless experience throughout the years. It means more to me than you know. Your listening and wanting to learn more about the subject encouraged and inspired me to keep working.

Thank you to my editor, Shayla Raquel. I'd be lost without you. Thank you for giving me direction. Thank you for both humbling me and pushing me to create the best book possible.

ABOUT THE AUTHOR
RICH HEBRON

 Rich Hebron is an American entrepreneur, public speaker, and author. He was raised in Raymond, Wisconsin, and lives in Chicago. He fuses both his rural and urban backgrounds to draw inspiration and to question the status quo. He continues challenging his perspective at morethanrich.co. Rich is an avid museum goer, dinosaur enthusiast, and NBA fan.

Connect with the Author

Visit morethanrich.co for more information.
Instagram: @richhebron
Twitter: @richhebron

Leave a Review

If you enjoyed this book, will you please consider writing a review on Amazon and Goodreads? Reviews help self-published authors make their books more visible to new readers.

Amazon: amazon.com/Homeless-but-Human-Life-Shelter-ebook/dp/B07H7ZG3FP

Goodreads: goodreads.com/book/show/41809699-homeless-but-human